Read Books All Day & Get Paid For It

The Business of Book Coaching

JENNIE NASH

Tree Farm Books
Santa Barbara, CA

Read Books All Day & Get Paid For It:
The Business of Book Coaching
Copyright © 2019 by Jennie Nash

Tree Farm Books
Santa Barbara, CA
www.jennienash.com

Printed in the United States of America

Cover designer: Stuart Bache
Designer: Carla Green

ISBN paperback 978-1-7332511-0-5
ISBN ebook 978-1-7332511-1-2

Contents

A Few Notes from the Author

Note #1: This is a book about making money as a book coach. I am a fan of making money, and I personally have made a lot of money as a book coach, but I would be remiss if I didn't make a strong plea for doing this work with integrity. In addition to making money, your goal should be to serve writers—to help them improve their craft, overcome their doubts, finish the books they start, and connect with readers. Our industry does not need any more people preying on the desperation of writers, offering get-rich-quick schemes, or write-an-instant-bestseller promises.

Note #2: I recommend a lot of books in this pages. It is, after all, a book about books! Links to all of these books, and many other resources, can be found on a list at jennienash.com/readbooksallday.

Note #3: In a few places in the text, I refer to Author Accelerator's Book Coach Training and Certification Program. This is an intensive and rigorous program I developed to teach people the actual work of book coaching. You can learn more about this program, as well as the comprehensive master class based on this book, at jennienash.com/readbooksallday.

PART 1
....
Becoming a Book Coach

The first book coach I ever had was my college room-mate, Bridget. Fate put us together in a tiny room in a remote freshman dorm—me, a tennis player/English major from Southern California, and she, a cheerleader/political science major from Maine—and for most of the rest of college, we never lived more than a few steps apart. Senior year, I hatched a scheme to write a series of linked narrative non-fiction pieces as an honors thesis. The topic was friendship—*our* friendship. I had to make sure Bridget was OK about my writing about everything I wanted to write about, so I would turn in my typewritten drafts to her long before my advisor ever saw them. She would respond and react to them, reflect back to me what was working and what wasn't, explain when I had gone too far in sharing a personal detail about her life, help me figure out a way around the hole when I took it out, ask me where the pages were when the pages weren't getting written, and cheer me on as the stack of finished pages grew.

She was an editor, coach, critic, trainer, judge, mirror, cheerleader, fan. She helped me do my best work and helped me become the kind of writer who sold her first book at the age of twenty-five. She read every page I wrote, even after I had an agent, even after I had an editor at a Big 5 publishing house.

I often use an exercise in my writing classes that I call the Universe of Support. It asks writers to make a target with two concentric circles. This gives them three spaces: an inner circle, middle circle, and exterior circle. I then ask the writers to place friends and family members in this universe according to exactly how much support each member gives to their writing. The only names that can go in the inner circle are the names of people who support the writer's work 100%.

What does 100% look like?

It looks like Bridget.

It looks like the boyfriend of one of my clients who was writing a moving memoir about being a gay phone-sex operator. After I'd been working with my client for about three months, his boyfriend called me. "I don't know what he is writing about or what you are doing to help," he said, "but I have never seen him so happy. I want to buy your coaching for him for six more months."

Sometimes people put their dogs in the inner circle.

Sometimes they put their dead mothers.

Sometimes they have no one to put in that sacred space, which is a tough realization, but also a good one because they can keep their writing away from the people who don't support it, and they can go out and find what they need: someone to support their writing life. Someone who wants them to succeed and helps them do their best work.

This is what a book coach does. Only instead of doing it for love, we do it as a professional in exchange for money.

Now it may seem odd that a writer would *pay* for this kind of support, when they can just get an awesome friend like Bridget—and that is, in fact, the subject of this book: How to be the person who gets paid to be like Bridget.

Or, as Ed Catmull says in *Creativity, Inc.*, how to wrestle with "the competing—but necessarily complementary—forces of art and commerce."

RECOMMENDED READING

» If you haven't already read ***Creativity, Inc.***, do it. This is one of my top recommendations for learning what it is like to systematize creativity—to develop a strategy around helping people do their best creative work. Each time I return to these pages, I learn something—how the Braintrust really works, what the rules for giving good feedback are, how not to crush the creative spirit, how a story develops over time in circular ways, and so much more.

The Problem with Free Help

The fact of the matter is that it's relatively easy for writers to get free help with their writing. They can go to a writers' meet-up, or a workshop, or a conference and make writer friends, or they can ask their college roommates, or their sisters, or their neighbor who is a seventh grade English teacher to read their pages.

But here is the terrible truth: Free help is not always good help. It *can* be, on occasion, and writers who have found a smart, supportive, fair-minded, tough, and kind critique partner or writers' group should hold on as tight as they can.

But free help is, in fact, often damaging help.

In my work as a book coach and as the CEO of Author Accelerator, a book-coaching company, I see this damage every day.

I see people who are mistakenly convinced that their work is pitch perfect and ready for publication because their writing friends told them for years that it was soooo good.

I see people whose pages have been batted around by their writing group to the point where their work reads as if it has been written by a committee.

I see people who keep giving their work to family members and friends who are way out of the center of their universe of support, and who give such mean-spirited and judgmental critiques that the writers become paralyzed with shame or fear or both.

People are generally too embarrassed to talk about their own experiences getting burned in this way—it feels so personal—but I hear a lot of writers telling harrowing stories about writer friends. I recently received this note from a writer who heard me speak about writing group damage:

> *"I just finished watching you [on a webinar] and what you said about writers' groups has always resonated with me--I've always avoided them because I think they're awful. But this last week, I started helping one of my writer buddies who went through a really awful experience last year with her critique group. It was horrible. It makes me so angry how mean people can be. She didn't tell me this until last week when I asked her how her writing was going and she said she hadn't written in a year. This is a friend with a whole fin-*

ished first draft. And this experience crushed her. She stopped writing, revising, dreaming."

What a book coach does is say to these writers, "You don't have to put up with that kind of abuse or lack of support. You are a good writer and you are worthy of this work. You can learn what you need to learn. Don't stop dreaming. Let me help you raise your voice and write the best book you can."

The Rise of the Book Coach

Book coaching is a profession that has emerged as a result of the changing forces in book publishing over the last decade. When mainstream publishers had a death grip on the means of production and distribution of books, when they were the gatekeepers and curators of every book that was made available to the public, the work of a book coach was done "in-house" by employees of the publishers. There was time to get each project ready for primetime, and time to nurture a writer's career.

Editors often purchased book projects that were not fully cooked. If a book and a writer showed promise, they would buy the book and then work with the writer to do what had to be done to get it into publishable shape. As a result, deep bonds formed between editors and writers, as the editors shepherded the writers' work to fruition—think Maxwell Perkins guiding F. Scott Fitzgerald and Hemingway, or Ursula Nordstrom guiding Maurice Sendak and E.B. White.

RECOMMENDED READING

» If you want a sense of what those days were like, read ***Dear Genius: The Letters of Ursula Nordstrom***. It takes you inside the famous editor's relationship with her famous writers—the day-to-day support she gave, the guidance, the tough love. It's a beautiful book.

The point of all this is that, back in the day, a writer's job was largely just to write. The myth of the lone genius in the attic or the garret was deeply entrenched in the lore of what it meant to be a writer, and the editor was the person who did everything else: got the work ready to publish, worked with the sales and marketing people, worked with the money people, worked with the cover artists, fielded requests for interviews, told the writer where and when it was time to speak to the public, and so on. Publishing was a business built on the hunches of these editors. Each "product" was a totally new thing, unlike, say, toothpaste or cars, which could be mass-produced. So the editors were charged with discerning what the reading public would buy. A blessing from them could turn the book into a mass-market hit and make the writer's entire career. They had absolute power to curate which books saw the light of day. Writers who were not chosen had no other option but to set their work aside and try again or take up some other creative endeavor.

Well, that's not entirely true. A person with enough money in the bank could go to a "vanity publisher," who would produce their book for a fee. These books were frowned upon by the entire industry because they had not been vetted and chosen.

This paradigm of the publishing industry was still largely in place when I graduated from college in 1986 and took a job working for two editors—one fiction and one nonfiction—at Ballantine Books, a division of Random House. Writers were still submitting their typed manuscripts through the mail. We had stacks and stacks of rubber band-bound manuscripts in manila padded envelopes in the office, towering so high they threatened to topple. I typed up the rejection letters my editor bosses had written by hand on yellow legal pads, typed out the writers' addresses on the envelopes, and took them to the mailroom.

That world is long gone.

Today, the majority of editors at traditional houses don't have time to nurture their writers. They juggle a huge number of titles in a fast-paced world hungry for the next hit. One former Big 5 editor I know told me she typically was responsible for thirty books every month. It's no wonder that editors and agents alike seem to be looking for projects that are fully baked and ready to go to press—with a built-in buying audience to boot.

That's why we see so many books by celebrities, Instagram stars, and prominent people from other industries: those books are guaranteed to sell. Writers wishing to compete in this environment and get a traditional deal must come into the process of pitching with highly polished work.

The advent of self-publishing has also made it possible for writers to skip the whole process of trying to get selected by agents and publishers and take their books directly to readers. This massive change means more opportunity for more writers to reach an audience, but the onus is on the writer to do all the work of a publisher. This means they either must work with a hybrid publisher who will take care of all the production details (for an upfront fee the writer pays) or they must assemble their own team of pros to get their work ready for primetime, which includes everything from cover artists to proofreaders.

Savvy writers in both the self-publishing and traditional publishing realms turn to book coaches to help them nurture their projects and their careers and to ensure that the writing they are doing is the best work they can do.

The Cost of the Dream

Why are writers so willing to invest in their writing life, when there are so many other pressing needs for their hard-earned dollars?

There are three main reasons I see come up over and over again:

1. The primary reason people give for wanting to write a book may surprise you. It's not to make money or make an impact or a name for themselves. It's not to impact an audience or spread a message. It's that *they don't want to die before they write their book*. They want to prove to themselves they can do it and prove to the naysayers that they can do it. They want to accomplish a thing that so many people *say* they want to do but so few actually *do*. It matters to them, deeply, which is why they are willing to invest in professional guidance to help them get there, even though they realize they may never make that money back.

2. Another reason I see come up again and again as a motivation for writing is that people want to raise their voice. They have been silenced by parents and partners and bosses, and they are tired of it. They want to stand up on a soapbox and speak their truth—whether their truth is about a topic they are expert in, or a story about dragons. Raising your voice is, again, not about selling books. It's about speaking up and speaking out, at long last, and it matters enormously to many writers. It is also a terrifying reality for them. When people are scared to finish or to publish, or when they are worried no one will like what they have written, it is often straight up fear of being seen and heard.

3. The third most common reason people want to write is that they want to make an impact. They are not writing for themselves. They don't want their words to end up in a drawer or buried on a hard drive. They want to connect with people, to change them, to influence the conversation. I like to say that connecting with a reader closes the loop for the writer. It completes the circuit. Without a reader, a writer is shouting in the dark. We want to *matter*—and that means having an impact on a reader.

To give you an idea what these reasons look like in real life, here are some examples of what Author Accelerator writers have said about working with their book coaches:

"'You'll never be Shakespeare,' my mother often told me as a girl. That, and dozens of other complicated cautions, kept me drawing safely within the writing

lines for years. When I decided to write my first book, I needed a coach who would not only know the writing and publishing business inside and out, but also understand, deeply, what drives people to write in the first place. I found that ideal combination in [my coach]. I was reminded of the value of these gifts this morning when I received notes back on a new chapter. I was writing about how my mother constantly reminded me that I would never be Shakespeare. 'If she had only lived to read this book, she'd be eating her words,' [my coach] replied. I laughed out loud and then cried for 15 minutes. Here was that 'Yes, you can!' encouragement that my ten-year-old self needed. And no, not to try to write like Shakespeare, but to continue to wholeheartedly write just like me: to write myself into the truth."

"It's absolutely invaluable to have feedback on your story as you're writing it. It helps silence those little voices that say, `Is this story worth writing? Am I the right person to write it? Have I completely lost my mind?'"

"For so many years, I wanted to write. I DID write, albeit sporadically. Not until I [started coaching] did I take up writing as a *practice*—and that has made all the difference in giving me a mindset as a writer."

What a book coach offers a writer is far more than just editorial support. We help them achieve a lifelong dream. It is critical for you to understand this. If you think you are only just helping a writer make their sentences prettier and their story or argument stronger, you are short-changing your contribution, and, as we will see later, that means you might also be short-changing your value and the money you are capable of making.

You are helping your clients complete a *transformation*. You are showing them how to go from someone who wants to write a book, who talks about it, who dreams of it, to someone who has created a book they are proud of.

That transformation is worth an enormous amount to a lot of writers. If you are going to open and run a business to help them do that, you need to first believe in the value yourself—and that you are capable of delivering it.

The Business of Being a Book Coach

In this book, I am going to guide you through the business of being a book coach. We are not talking here about *how* to do it—I have an entire program for that—The Book Coach Training and Certification Program at Author Accelerator. This book is about how to set up a successful, sustainable coaching business that will serve your stated audience, and bring you good money and a sense of satisfaction. It is designed to help people new to book coaching as well as people who are already running a coaching practice and want to level-up their game.

I have been a book coach for more than ten years now. I make multiple six figures a year from this work and I also run a book-coaching company that offers a lot of other coaches good, satisfying work. But I am never going to promise you that you can make as much money as I do, or that you can make enough to quit your day job, or put your kids through college, or even buy a great new pair of shoes, because running a business of any kind does not come with any guarantees. It takes hard work to build a business, to sustain it, to grow it. It takes an entrepreneurial mindset—and maybe you don't have that inborn sense of hustle.

I see so many offers on the internet from successful business, career, or life coaches who promise you can make what they are making, and these offers make me crazy because they feel so manipulative. Can a mom with a full-time job who is working part-time as a book coach expect to make six figures her first year as a coach? Of course not. Can someone who doesn't want to be on social media, doesn't want to optimize their website, doesn't want to invest in their success make six figures? Of course not.

What I *can* promise you is that I will share what I have figured out along the way about running a successful coaching business and teach you what I have learned in my own business and as CEO of the coaching team at Author Accelerator.

PART 2

. . . .

The Business of Book Coaching

There are an endless number of ways to find clients for your book-coaching business because there are so many people who want to write a book. Some experts claim writing a book is a dream for up to 80% of Americans. I'm not sure about the validity of that number, but I do know this: *almost without exception*, when I meet people and tell them I am a book coach, they reply that they have always wanted to write a book, or their mother is writing a book, or their girlfriend, or their neighbor, or the guy that sits next to them at work. No one ever stares at me blankly and says, "I don't know any-one who wants to write a book."

Chatting with random strangers will prove to you that a lot of people want to write a book, but you can't run a book-coaching business off of these strangers. You need to be intentional about who you want to serve, how you want to serve them, where you can find them, what you will charge for your services, and what services you will offer.

In this section, I will answer all of these questions.

The 9 Business Channels for Book Coaching

Before we dig into specifics, let's define the book-coaching universe. There are nine main business channels where you can work as a book coach. Read through them and get a sense of the range of ways you can help people reach their book-writing goals.

1. **1:1 Coaching—online.** You can run your own online book-coaching business where you use digital tools to advertise your business, connect with clients, and conduct your business.
2. **1:1 Coaching—in person.** You can run your own book-coaching business where you only work face-to-face with clients.
3. **Workshops.** You can coach clients in groups through short-term online or in-person workshops.
4. **Writing retreats.** You can coach clients on retreats, which tend to be longer and more intensive than workshops and are often held in exotic locations where you might want to travel.
5. **Coaching company.** You can become a coach for a company like Author Accelerator that hires book coaches to work in their system and delivers clients to you.
6. **Local college, university, and continuing ed centers.** You can coach writers by teaching or mentoring at institutions of higher learning.
7. **Writing centers.** You can coach writers by teaching or mentoring at centers whose sole purpose is to help writers.
8. **Writing conferences.** You can teach or mentor writers through writing conferences that exist to help writers sharpen their skills and prepare their work for publication.

9. **Pitch contests.** You can mentor writers through contests whose mission is to prepare writers to pitch to agents. While this is not typically a way to earn money as a book coach, it is a way to gain experience and exposure, and so I am including it on the list.

> **Take Action**
> Which channels interest you the most? Write them down with some brief notes about why those channels are the ones that get your attention.

Defining Who You Want to Serve

In order to begin to focus your book-coaching business, you need to think about what kind of coaching you want to do, which means you need to think about what kind of client you might best serve.

There are generally three ways to categorize the writers who you will find in all those business channels, above:

1. **Genre.** This is the most obvious way for a book coach to categorize writers, and many coaches focus their business by serving writers of a particular genre. There are many excellent reasons to focus in this way, including the fact that it is easier to market yourself within one genre and easier to gain mastery.

    Marion Roach Smith is a perfect example of this kind of book coach. She has built a very successful business around coaching memoir and offering a wide variety of services for memoir writers, including a book, courses, workshops, and coaching. She is well-known for her work and well-respected for it.

Another example is Cathy Yardley (*RockYourWriting*.com), who focuses on genre fiction.

Note that genre is not the only way to organize a successful business. In my business, for example, I coach a wide range of genres. At the moment, I am coaching writers working in memoir, in fiction ranging from YA fantasy to historical fiction to women's fiction, and in self-help ranging from business leadership to a book about parenting. What unites my clients are the next two categories.

2. **Level.** A beginning writer will have needs that are different than those of a more seasoned writer. Beginning writers may have a lot of questions about craft and the publishing industry in general, whereas seasoned writers may need more assistance on structure, rate of production (how to write better, faster), and managing doubt. (Yes, doubt tends to get worse, not better, as a writer progresses in their career.)

You may decide to focus your business on writers at a particular level. In my work, for example, I do not coach beginning writers—meaning those who need basic craft assistance or a lot of explanation about the way the industry works. My clients tend to be operating at a very high level, even if they have never written a book before. They might have deep writing experience as a teacher, a lawyer, or a PR professional, and need assistance on managing the complex project of a book.

Book coach Lisa Tener is on the staff of the Harvard Medical School Publishing Conference and is known for her excellent work serving doctors, therapists, and others in the medical, healthcare, and self-help world. She has carved out a niche for her business at the intersection of genre and level: Most of her clients are seasoned experts in their field who are writing nonfiction but who have never written a book before.

3. **Goal.** Not every writer is going to know what their publishing goal is, but you can organize your coaching business around certain common goals, including these three general ones:

- Writing a book in order to impact readers, establish oneself as a thought leader in an industry, and make money.

  Writers with this goal might seek an agent and a traditional publishing deal, or they might choose to work with a hybrid publisher or self-publish. Within this category there are a great number of ways to serve writers, including helping them determine their publishing path, helping them structure their books, helping them write their books, helping them prepare book proposals and agent pitches, and helping them with production (including copyediting and proofreading), marketing, and book launching.

  My clients are all aiming go have the greatest possible number of readers, so they would fall into this category.

Note that when coaching nonfiction book proposals, I guide writers in the development of robust marketing plans, but I do not help them *execute* their marketing plans and book launches. I have had many writers ask me to help them do this work, but I have drawn that line in my business and do not cross over it. I have colleagues and other experts I send people to for this kind of coaching. Some book coaches take writers all the way through the entire process.

- Completing a book as a personal accomplishment in order to leave a legacy or fulfill a dream regardless of whether it gets published.

I know a woman, Loren Stephens, who runs a thriving business at *WriteWisdom.com* helping older people capture their life story in a memoir to share with their families. They are not interested in being published by Penguin Random House, getting their books into airport bookstores, or appearing on stage in front of a large audience of readers and fans, but they want to hold their book in their hands, and she helps them do that.

- Writing as a path to awakening and understanding oneself and the world.

My friend Jen Louden has for many years run a thriving community called Weekly Oasis, which is focused on helping writers find their voice and reclaim their creative desires. She helps them dig deep into their reasons for not writing and helps them overcome resistance and stay focused. Some of her audience goes on to write books, but that is not their primary goal.

You can see there are many ways to serve writers at various parts of the writing process. The key to running a successful business is knowing who you will serve—and who you won't, which we will discuss next.

> **Take Action**
> Which category of writer interests you the most? Why? Write some brief notes about why those categories interest you.

Deciding Who You WON'T Serve

I had a huge breakthrough in my own book-coaching business when I wrote a manifesto about who I would *not* serve. I did this under the tutelage of digital strategist Sarah Avenir, in a course she taught about leading what she called "a small nation" or tribe of people. She described a business as being a lighthouse on a hill on an island. You shine your light and the people who need you will find you.

To write the manifesto about who you won't serve, Sarah suggested thinking about who you would kick off your island, and why.

Your "will not serve" list might include people from the categories and channels we just discussed, or it might include things such as the topic they are writing about or the time zone they live in or even what industry they work in for their "real" job. I can imagine a business focused on lawyers who want to write fiction, for example, which would mean you would not serve fashion designers and veterinarians. This narrowing of focus would allow you to tailor your programs to what lawyers know about story.

This kind of focusing happens all over the publishing industry.

- An agent I know focuses on Christian writers and will not take on books that have gratuitous sex, human-divine physical relationships, and other elements antithetical to a Christian reader.
- At Author Accelerator, we take time zone into account when matching writers and coaches, because we've found it can harm the overall coaching relationship if they have difficulty finding a time they're both available for phone calls.
- I personally can't work with horror writers because horror scares me too much.

Be sure that your "will not serve" list also takes into consideration the behavior or personality of clients.

At one point in my career, I did an assessment of the clients who were bringing me the most joy and the most money. I learned that the men I was serving were causing me more anxiety than the women. I was so surprised by this outcome that I dug into the reason why this was so, and analyzed who these men were, what they were writing, and how they had come into my coaching practice.

I learned there was a moment in my client-intaking process when I was falling prey to a bad little habit. Many men would question why I was charging what I charged. They would, in effect, ask me to prove my worth. I would take on this challenge and find a big thrill in convincing them. It felt like winning a battle. It felt awesome to turn someone's opinion around. But over time, I learned that people who need to be convinced are not my ideal clients. So it wasn't men who were the problem; it was people who needed to be convinced. I raised my awareness around this idea, defined my ideal customer in a more nuanced way, and now happily serve a great number of men who bring me joy—and money.

At Author Accelerator, we developed a list of the seven kinds of problematic writers, because when running a large organization like ours, we frequently deal with them, and knowing who they are and how they act helps us recognize them faster and deal with them better—or avoid serving them in the first place. In a business where you are the sole coach, you may want to shut these kinds of writers out completely:

1. Writers who are a plain-old bad fit
2. Writers who are pushy
3. Writers who make excuses
4. Writers who are too in love with their own work
5. Writers who are too attached to a particular method of writing
6. Writers who are combative
7. Writers who are rude, condescending, mean-spirited, upsetting, or unreasonably demanding

You can read more about each of these kinds of writers and how to handle them at *jennienash.com/readbooksallday* and think about which kinds of writers you can tolerate and which you cannot.

Be honest with yourself, but also be realistic. Writers can be extremely passionate, extremely needy, and extremely emotional. This is why they often write things that are deeply important and moving to others. It's part of the work of a book coach to help writers manage all parts of the project, including the personality and behavioral issues.

Take Action
What kind of writer will you refuse to serve? Write out your thoughts.

Digging Deeper: Defining Your Tribe

When I was in Sarah Avenir's course, I wrote a few pages about the writers I knew I wouldn't serve, and the act of defining that helped me define who I would. It was a fledgling effort, and over the years, I continue to refine this with every new client and every new project.

A few years ago, a writer who is himself a coach—an executive business coach—asked me to explain how I select the writers I work with. "How do you know when you engage with a writer that they will be the perfect fit for you?" he asked. "How can you tell if their personality and style will be a good match for you? How can you tell that they will be the type of person you can't wait to work with each week and that helping them along their journey will make you better?"

He asked these insightful questions because he had a keen understanding of the way the coaching relationship works, and when it tends to be the most successful. In hiring his own coach, he wanted to be sure he was choosing well.

My answer became the latest version of my manifesto on both who I will and will not work with:

I have reached a point in my career where I am able to choose who to work with. I base my choice on a number of factors.

1. *Is the project commercially viable? I want to help writers who want to reach the maximum possible number of readers, and there are some projects that are more likely to do that than others. I have a pretty good nose for that, by this point—although that doesn't mean there are any guarantees in publishing. There are not.*

    That being said, I do elect to work on projects that have a more modest external goal. I have been working for a year with a client, for example, who is retired after a long and distinguished career in Washington. She wanted to learn how to play the cello and how to write a novel. I admired her resolve, her seriousness of purpose, her intention, and her passion for the inner workings of politics (which is what her story is about) and accepted her as a client on those strengths. It has been one of the most satisfying coaching relationships I have had. At the start, I would have put the odds of her being traditionally published at about zero. Now, however, they are probably more than 50%.

    I am not the coach for clients who want to write simply because it feels good, or because they enjoy it, or because their friends tell them they have such interesting stories to tell. There is nothing wrong with those intentions, but I can't have a significant enough impact on those projects to make it worth my time.

2.   *Is the writer coachable? Are they ready, willing, and able to accept guidance? Can they take what I have to offer? Are they going to listen when I suggest starting over, throwing out pages, doing another revision of their 300-page book? This may be the most important criterion.*

3.   *Do they have a fire in their belly? Writing a book is a long, hard, complex, and emotionally difficult undertaking and everyone has demands on their time, doubt in their mind, and any number of other potential roadblocks to success. Persistence is far more important than talent, so I try to get a sense of why they are doing this, what they hope to get from it, and whether or not they have the resolve to see it through. This may be the most important criterion—side-by-side with #2.*

4.   *Related to numbers 1 and 3 is this: Are they willing to do what it takes to reach readers? These are the skills I was referring to that entrepreneurs have honed better than writers. Many writers have what it takes to write but they refuse to engage on social media, don't like public speaking, don't want to learn what they need to manage a website or host a webinar, and hate it when I talk about ideal readers, target audiences, and marketing plans. Writers can no longer "just write." It may be a sad reality but it's a reality, nonetheless. If I encounter someone who refuses to be open to these other demands, their odds of success (reaching readers)*

will be greatly diminished and their odds of being satisfied with the coaching process will decrease.

5. *Can they afford my fees? Publishing is a gamble. Working with a book coach is an investment that may or may not pay off. I couldn't work with someone who didn't understand that, or who was demanding some kind of monetary ROI.*

6. *Will working with this writer make me a better person? That's a critical criterion, too. I am absolutely made better by working with my clients and I look forward to opening their submission emails every day. I love my work—and the vast majority of my clients end up being my friends. I have many clients who have worked with me for many years—we are now on second and third books. I have become a better editor, a better coach, a better writer, and a better person by my association with these people.*

    If I encounter someone who is NOT going to offer that potential, I sever the relationship. I just did this last week, with a client whom I had misjudged in a number of the important ways I have just outlined. It doesn't happen often, but it happens. It just means there is a better coach or teacher or way forward for that person.

CJ McClanahan, the writer who asked me the question that resulted in that manifesto, called my reply "the best email I've read all year." He signed up to work with me, and finished and published his book, *The Overachiever's Dilemma*, which he uses in workshops and consulting gigs. CJ also referred another client to me the following year, one of *his* clients, who also finished and published his book. Knowing very clearly who I will and won't serve helps me run a better business.

Take Action
Write a fully fleshed out manifesto about who you will and will not serve.

RECOMMENDED READING

» ***Gather the People*** by Sarah Avenir. This book explains Sarah's ideas about defining and serving an audience in a way that is authentic and effective. The book is incredibly helpful for anyone who is struggling with this step, nervous about it, unsure, worried, or just plain stuck. I found it to be very inspiring.

» ***Tribes*** by Seth Godin. This is a short and powerful little book about stepping up to lead a tribe of people—to take charge, take the helm, be the person others rally around. It's about having a vision and sharing it. I will be mentioning other Seth Godin books throughout our discussion of running a book-coaching business because he is one of the most respected and effective marketing experts around. I'm a fan!

Defining Your Mission

Once you know the category of writer you wish to serve and the type of writer you will and won't serve, you need to do some work to figure out *how* you will serve them. This means first thinking about the ways writers tend to experience pain.

Please note that the list I am sharing here only encompasses the pain writers may experience while *writing*. The moment a book goes into production, either through self-publishing or traditional publishing or something in between, is the moment when a thousand other points of pain come into the process, such as designing the cover, setting the price, planning the launch, dealing with reviews, facing fans and critics, and managing sales—but I am concerned here only with the writing phase of the process.

And just to be clear, I do not believe that the process of writing and publishing a book is all about pain. I also believe it is infused with deep satisfaction and soaring joy. But pain is what tends to get people to act and when you are selling a service for writers, you want them to act.

Here are the four most common kinds of writerly pain I see and some thoughts for how a book coach can help a writer through them.

1. **The writer doesn't know how to start their book.** I see a lot of writers who have a great idea and talk with great enthusiasm about bringing it to life, but they get stuck before they even start. They often write the same opening chapter over and over and over again. They never really commit; they never move forward. They may spend a great deal of time going to conferences and workshops, but they never actually move out of the starting gate.

This problem of paralysis at the beginning of a project is often a fear of creative commitment. After all, if a writer decides to write *one* book idea, it means they're not writing another. They are choosing THIS book, with all its flaws and imperfections.

And as soon as the writer chooses, they are taking a risk that the thing they make won't be as shiny and perfect as the thing in their head. They are moving out of the realm of imagined perfection and into the realm of—well, everything less than imagined perfection. It's an uncomfortable place to be. So rather than suffer the discomfort of action, they choose the discomfort of inaction.

A book coach can:

- Help a writer take action simply by committing to the project
- Help a writer build their confidence by providing a safe back-and-forth
- Help a writer define their book through the Blueprint for a Book process that I teach in the Advanced Book Coach Training course, or another process for laying a strong foundation
- Help a writer decide they don't actually want to write the book they think they want to write

2. **The writer doesn't know how to finish their draft.** They get ten or twenty chapters in, and then they lose interest. Or they get close to the end and decide what they have written is garbage. Or they decide they don't actually have the time it will take to bring their book to life. Or they give their fragile pages to the one person who

is guaranteed to say the worst possible judgmental and horrible things, which gives the writer permission to put the work away and never finish. They spend a lot of time on their writing, but they never actually finish.

The reason for this inertia is usually straight-up fear. The writer is afraid of failing or afraid of succeeding, which is to say they are afraid of something that might happen in the future.

A book coach can:

- Help a writer stop giving work to people who are punishing them
- Help a writer stop focusing on an imagined future and focus on the work instead
- Help a writer define their fear so they can better understand it
- Help a writer form the habits necessary to work regardless of how they feel
- Help a writer build their muscle for discerning when the story is working or not

3. **The writer doesn't know how to revise their book.** They get to the end of a draft and have a party to celebrate the milestone. It is, after all, a massively big milestone, and a party is certainly warranted. But then they get paralyzed about what to do next. All they feel is overwhelm (What do I do now?) and doubt (Is this even any good?), and their response is to go back to the pages and endlessly fiddle with the sentences. Or they seek out beta-readers and endlessly fuss about the feedback they get.

A book coach can:
- Help a writer discern what is working in the manuscript
- Help a writer with a project plan for revision
- Help a writer prioritize the elements to work on
- Help a writer by bringing an expert's outside perspective to the work

4. **The writer doesn't know when to enter the marketplace.** They do something obviously harmful such as send out their still-rough draft to agents just to "test the waters" and rack up folders full of rejections. Or they rush to self-publish and end up with a total readership of 20 friends.

Or they do the opposite: They spend years and years polishing their pages, making every sentence shine, but it's all really just a cleverly disguised way to procrastinate and ensure that they will never actually send it out into the world.

The goal at this stage of the process is to focus on producing what I call a good enough draft. A good enough draft is a draft that helps the writer reach their publishing goal, which means they have to know their publishing goal.

- Are they self-publishing a series where the most important thing their readers want is the next book? Their good enough draft is a draft that is done when they promised their readers it would be done.
- Are they working with a hybrid publisher who will only offer proofreading of their pages and no other

editing? Their good enough draft should be almost camera-ready—ready to go to press—as perfect as they can make it (without using perfection as an excuse for procrastination).

- Are they writing a nonfiction book to help them become a thought leader in their industry? Their good enough draft is a draft their beta-readers are begging to share with their friends.
- Are they trying to land an agent and a traditional publishing deal? Their good enough draft is the one that will get an agent's attention, which is to say they have an idea that is commercially viable, and they have proven they can execute it well enough for a national audience. It might still need a bit of work—maybe a new introduction, some work to refine the middle, a better title—but it is solid, whole, vibrant, and marketable. The goal in this situation, in other words, is not to be ready to go to press. The goal is to impress the agents and editors.

A book coach can:
- Help a writer define their publishing goals
- Help a writer choose a publishing path
- Help a writer discern when their draft is good enough
- Help a writer polish their pages
- Help a writer manage beta-reader feedback
- Help a writer strategize how to pitch
- Help a writer develop a pitch
- Help a writer navigate the pitch process

RECOMMENDED READING

» I wrote *The Writer's Guide to Agony and Defeat: The 47 Worst Moments in the Writing Life and How to Get Over Them* to help writers through the toughest parts of the work of writing a book worth reading. It discusses all the pain points, and how to move past them.

» To learn more about writerly pain, I also recommend *Bird by Bird* by Anne Lamott, because, of course. And *The War of Art* by Stephen Pressfield and *Art and Fear* by David Bayles and Ted Orland, two other classics.

Take Action

Answer the following questions:
- At which pain point do you believe you can have the most impact as a book coach?
- How can you have an impact? In other words, what can you do to help writers get over their problem or their pain?
- What qualities or characteristics do you bring to the work that could add value for these kinds of writers? In order to answer this question, review the **Characteristics of an Effective Book Coach** on the next page. These are the characteristics I see in people who tend to become good book coaches. Which of these can you leverage to help the kinds of writers you wish to help? Write about any of the characteristics you possess and how you believe they will help you.

Characteristics of an Effective Book Coach

1. **They love books.** They love to read. They are the kinds of people who stayed up late reading under the covers with a flashlight as a kid. They think a great day includes curling up with a great book. They love to talk about books, to read reviews, to haunt bookstores.

2. **They love writers.** They admire the work writers do and appreciate what it takes to sit alone in a room long enough to produce a book-length work. They understand that people who yearn to write often feel emotions very deeply. They understand that when a writer shares their work, they are sharing a piece of their soul.

3. **They feel comfortable with the creative process.** They understand the iterative nature of creativity and the fact that getting to a finished project is never a straightforward path. They know that beauty can arise from chaos.

4. **They feel confident managing a complex project.** They have the ability to think logically and strategically about both the story and the creative process. They can give clear direction about how to proceed with a project so that it stays on point and on track to meeting the writer's goals.

5. **They have the ability to focus on details and on the big picture—often at the same time.** Great book coaches see the small things on the page and the big things about the way the book will live in the world. They are excellent at making connections between ideas and concepts and can even see things that *aren't* there.

6. **They understand the marketplace.** They understand books are products that get bought and sold, that publishers—either traditional publishers or individual self-published writers—want to make money on the books they sell. They understand readers are very discerning and have a choice whether or not they will read any given book.

7. **They like to work 1:1.** Book coaching is not the kind of work you can do at a distance. You have to lean into the writer's mind and their world, which means you also have to figure out how to establish boundaries so you don't get sucked into places where you are not trained to work, and where a therapist would be better suited.

8. **They like to work alone.** Editing is done alone in a room. Even if you are in a coffee shop or a library with other people who are working, you are alone in your head. You need to enjoy that.

9. **They have the ability to step back from the emotion to protect themselves from getting too drawn in.** It's hard to run a solid business if you get caught up in a writer's drama. You need to be able to be part of their creative process, but stand apart from it, as well.

10. **They are self-motivated.** They can meet deadlines, prioritize their work, and keep projects moving along without anyone telling them they need to do it.

Write a Mission Statement

You now have all the elements you need to write a coherent mission statement to describe your book coaching business. The idea here is something short and sweet you could use on a Facebook page or website; something you could say in response to the question, "What do you do?"

Be sure your answer is really about *you*—what unique thing you do, and in what unique way you do it, and for which intentionally chosen audience.

I don't believe mission statements should be something you do once and never look at again. I believe they are living, breathing statements that change as you change and grow as you grow. You don't, therefore, have to be scared of this step. Just write what you are feeling now, what you believe reflects your business goals now. If it changes after a few more chapters in this book, or in a few months, or next year, that's fine.

And if you are already running a coaching business and are here to level up your game, you might consider reviewing your mission statement and making sure it aligns with the work you want to be doing.

Here is my mission statement, which, to prove the point I just made, I recently updated:

I get into writers' heads and, using a potent mix of tough love, proven strategy, and book-seeing super powers, challenge them to write books worth reading. I serve fiction and nonfiction writers who are serious about making a big impact in either traditional or independent publishing, and who are ready, able, and willing to invest in their success with their time, energy, heart, and money.

Take Action
Write out a complete mission statement for your business. Keep in mind this doesn't have to be your mission statement forever. The best business owners periodically reflect on their statement and change it as their business changes. You can keep coming back to yours in the same way.

Consider the Competition

Once you know your mission, you can research the competition. Who else is serving these kinds of writers? We ask this so we can establish ourselves in the marketplace in a way that allows us to stand out and be effective.

Just asking these questions, however, sends many would-be coaches into a tailspin, because it's where the idea of running a business becomes less theoretical and all too real. You will see other book coaches out there who were senior executives at publishing imprints such as Hyperion and Little Brown. You will see coaches who are themselves *New York Times* bestselling writers and whose clients are megawatt stars.

Helping writers bring their books to life sounds sort of dreamy and wonderful but talking about other coaches and the whole idea of competitive businesses sounds a little frightening. It brings up all those tough questions such as, "Who am I to guide other writers when I haven't even published one of my own books?" or "What if no one wants to pay me for my help?"

These are legitimate concerns, but my intention with this book is to help you gain confidence in your ability to run a successful coaching business. *Coaching is a learnable skill and it is a different skill than being able to write, publish and market a book of your own.* By understanding the landscape in which you are doing business and what you can offer that is of value, you'll be in a better position to value your contribution and believe in your worth.

RECOMMENDED READING

» ***You Are a Badass*** by Jen Sincero. This is the most self-helpy of self-help books, and it has a definite "if you can dream it, you can manifest it" mentality (which doesn't jive so well with someone who believes in intention and strategy), but it's so full of hope and promise and can-do spirit that it has its place if you need a kick in the pants.

» ***The Big Leap*** by Gay Hendricks. This book has some flaws: it's a bit repetitive; it lacks actionable steps in certain sections; and as with Sincero's book, there is also a strong dose of ***The Secret*** in it. But the concept of the limiting beliefs we put on ourselves, and how to break through those beliefs, is explained in a way that is very easy to see and grasp, and that idea is SO important. If you are hoping to become a coach who guides others to achieve their dreams, I think it's important to do some work on your own mindset about dreams and goals too.

Take Action

Look at the nine business channels we mentioned in Part 2 to unearth the big players in the field. Aim to study at least ten individuals or organizations. Make a grid to organize the information. You can download an example and a template at jennienash.com/readbooksallday

Ask yourself these questions:
- *How are these organizations guiding writers to success? What services are they offering?*
- *What are they charging?*
- *How long do writers tend to work with them?*
- *Are their services effective for the writers? Are they delivering on their promise?*
- *Is their business model effective as a business enterprise? Do they seem to be doing well? What evidence do you have for this?*

Once you have your grid, answer the following questions:
- *Which of the businesses on your list are most aligned with what you want to do? Why?*
- *Which ones make you green with envy? Why?*
- *How can you offer something different than what they are offering? What can you bring to the mix that is unique? You may not yet know completely since we have not yet worked on pricing or packaging, but it's good to take a stab at it at this stage of the process. Just quickly brainstorm what services you might offer, how you might price them, how quickly you might deliver them, and in what format you might deliver them.*

Put your offerings on the grid to line them up with the competition.

Naming Your Values—How You Will Do Business

You're not finished defining your business until you can define HOW you are going to do business. What are the values that are going to drive you? It's so critical to ask and answer these questions because when things get hard in business—and they will get hard—you are going to want a set of guidelines to direct your actions. Instead of making things up at every turn, you can say, "I will make this decision based on my values."

It may seem easy to reel off a set of values you believe in—e.g., respect, fairness, compassion, diversity, quality, equity, courage, environmental stewardship, simplicity, service, accessibility, accountability—but what's hard is understanding what those words really mean to you in terms of how you conduct yourself. It's important to narrow them down and rank them, so you know what comes first and why. That is the work that allows your values to guide your business.

Here are the core values of a few well-known companies, courtesy of the *6Q Blog*. If you're familiar with the company, you should be able to read them and think, *YES, that makes total sense.*

Facebook
- Focus on impact
- Move fast
- Be bold
- Be open
- Build social value

Ikea

- Humbleness and willpower
- Leadership by example
- Daring to be different
- Togetherness and enthusiasm
- Cost-consciousness
- Constant desire for renewal
- Accept and delegate responsibility

Starbucks Coffee

- Creating a culture of warmth and belonging, where everyone is welcome.
- Acting with courage, challenging the status quo and finding new ways to grow our company and each other.
- Being present, connecting with transparency, dignity and respect.
- Delivering our very best in all we do, holding ourselves accountable for results.

Integrity

My core business values, which are as much of a work in progress as my mission statement, are as follows:

- Work with *integrity* at all times in all ways
- *Delight* the customer by taking their work as seriously as if it was my own
- Be *generous* to clients, colleagues, and members of the literary community
- Be *confident* in my powers, in my worth, and in my limitations

My highest value as a business owner and a book coach, as you can see, is integrity.

This plays out in a variety of ways in my business every day. I vow to tell my clients the truth, to be as honest as I can possibly be about what I am seeing in their ideas and their pages. This is part of my messaging in my client-facing communications, and it is also part of my behavior. I don't pull any punches—and sometimes that can be gut-wrenching for the writer and for me.

A well-known, multi-bestselling writer once came to me for help working in a genre that was new to him. He showed me a finished manuscript, and it was a mess, right from the start. I read it several times over to confirm my understanding of it, and really thought the whole thing should be scrapped. I thought he should start over with a different format. I went through days of doubt—*Who am I to tell him this news? It's just my opinion. What do I know anyway? What if I'm wrong?* But then I recommitted to my value of integrity and reminded myself this is why writers come to me. This is what I am offering. This is the foundation of my value.

So I told him my truth.

He didn't want to hear it, of course—no one does. But he was open to the conversation, he engaged in a dialogue, and together we discovered a way forward for him. It resulted in a very good outcome: he dug in, figured out what he really wanted to write, and pivoted in that direction.

Integrity also means sometimes talking people out of working with me. I am constantly telling customers that there is no guarantee with the investment they make in working with me, that they might not earn back the money, and that they have to be prepared to make nothing. I probably work harder to talk people out of working with me than I do to talk them into it. I only want to work with people who don't need to be talked into it.

Integrity guides everything I do.

And what is wonderful and fascinating to me is how often that value is reflected in the testimonials I get, and the thanks I receive, and the things people say when they explain why they recommended me and my programs to other people. There is a direct correlation between the way I conduct myself and the value people perceive to be getting from my business offerings.

This is one of the key reasons why I get referrals and repeat clients, and why I attract the right kinds of clients for me. Integrity is a cornerstone of my business success.

My other core values are also extremely important to the way I work—and sometimes they point to the weaknesses of my business, too. I like to be generous, but I can be generous to a fault. I offer clients special favors, extra little deadlines, quick reads of things that never turn out to be quick. Multiply that kind of generosity by five or ten, and, well, you can imagine what happens. I not only do this with clients, I do it with strangers. I recently met a young writer at a conference who had a killer idea and I offered her three months of low-priced coaching; she would never have been able to pay my prices and I was dying to help her get her book into an agent's hands. Because of my value of generosity, I often find myself working very late on weekdays or on the weekends to deliver on everything I promised—and that crushes my own energy and mojo, which means I can't help anyone. It is a constant balancing act, and I am far from doing it as well as I would like. Knowing my values, however, and being aware of how they play out in real time, is one of the ways I help keep my business on track.

Take Action
What are the core values that will guide your work?

We will put your income numbers, audience definitions and core values into a business plan in Part 6, but before we are ready to do that, we need to talk about money.

PART 3

How to Make Money

People are drawn to book coaching because they love books and stories and writers. They could lose themselves for days in libraries and bookstores, and their idea of heaven is talking all day with writers. There is a myth in our culture about the starving artist—the person who suffers greatly for their art—and this sometimes extends to people who help artists.

It is not noble to give away your time and talent without asking for money in return. I want to make sure you shake off the myth of the starving artist—the idea that writers can't pay for help or that you aren't worthy of being paid to help them. There are plenty of writers who can pay and are eager to pay, and if you can help them on their journey to bring their vision to life, you are worthy of being paid—and paid well.

How Much Money Do You Want to Make?

In the very early days of my freelance writing career, when I had first one and then two small children and had decided to work from home as a freelance magazine writer, my husband, Rob, would ask me each year what I planned to make. He is a finance guy with an MBA who was trying to create a family budget and it was a reasonable request, but I would always answer, "Zero." I believed that if I had very low expectations, anything I made would feel like a victory. This answer totally let me off the hook—no expectations, no pressure.

But, of course, Rob wouldn't take zero for an answer. He has always believed in me and my abilities far more than I believed in myself. Years after this, we would build a budget together that allowed me to take a year off to write my first novel. When I wanted to begin working with a high-priced business coach but felt nervous about the expenditure, he would say, "You'll earn it back." Whenever I freak out about hiring a new employee, he calmly says, "You have to spend money to make money." His belief in me and what I am doing is a huge reason I have been able to accomplish everything I have accomplished.

But back then, out of defiance and out of fear, I would give a very low yearly income goal. I would say, "Fine. $5,000."

And for a few years, that's about what I made, and that was the end of the conversation.

Then one year when the girls were both in school, Rob laid down a challenge: "You need to stop short-changing yourself," he said. "You're making way more than the goal you're setting. If you set a higher bar, odds are good you'll make it."

I swung the other direction that year and set a number nearly double what I had ever made as a freelancer. It felt a bit reckless, but I simply pitched more stories, proposed more ideas, risked more rejection. And lo and behold, I made the number.

As an entrepreneur, you are in charge of your fate. You get to decide how much you want to make, and then figure out a way to make it. You get to put a number down and make a plan for achieving it.

I find that a lot of writers, like artists and musicians, don't value their work as much as they should. We are quick to diminish it, to diminish ourselves. We are quick to think we aren't worthy. In addition to the fear of asking for what we want, we also tend to fear getting it. It took me years to get over these fears in my business, and I don't believe I would have hit the $100,000 or $200,000 mark in my coaching business if I hadn't done this work. It is, in fact, an ongoing struggle.

I urge you to do some journaling around your relationship to money, to read some books on it, and, if you need to, get some help. There are business coaches and money mindset coaches who could be very helpful in this regard, and well worth the investment.

RECOMMENDED READING

» *You Are a Badass at Making Money* by Jen Sincero—yup, her again. Same pros and same cons, but if you need to look at your lifelong relationship with money, the habits you learned from your family, the reasons you either do or don't value yourself, the excuses you are making, and the fantasies you are harboring about money, this is a powerful read.

» *The $100 Startup* by Chris Guillebeau. I love this book about starting a business. It breaks things down in such a way that makes everything seem do-able—and it is! It's also inspiring because there are many stories about people just like you and me, who took their dreams and brought them to life.

To get clear about money in your coaching business, you have to pick a number you want to make. If you are starting a book coaching business as a side hustle to a full-time job or other responsibilities, your number will be lower than if you are going all in. For the sake of argument, let's say the side-hustle coach wants to take home $1,500 a month, or $18,000 a year. And let's say the book coach going all in wants to take home $5,000 a month, or $60,000 a year.

Your mileage is going to vary. I have worked for myself for more than thirty years, as a freelance writer, a book coach, and an entrepreneur. There were those years I mentioned before when I made about $5,000 total and was happy to do so. In recent years, I have made multiple six figures from my book-coaching business.

People ask me what I think they can expect to make as a book coach, and if they have to have _____ in order to make any money at it. The blank varies, but it usually has something to do with external measures of success like a college degree, an agent, a published book, or a certain number of sales from said book. I'm not going to pretend those things don't matter, because, of course, they matter. But the good news about book coaching is that they don't matter as much as you might think. If you can effectively help writers with their pain, you can make money.

I have coaches working for me at Author Accelerator who are not published, and who have not even written a book. I have coaches working for me who do not have a college degree, who are raising children, or have severe physical disabilities, and they are all very good at what they do, and they are all making money.

The business of writer education is enormous. Although there is not a lot of data to prove it, all you have to do is look at how many writers go to conferences and workshops and retreats, and how many buy courses and video trainings and books. People are spending money to learn about writing. At Author Accelerator, we did a small poll to gather some data. Close to half of those we polled spent more than $10,000 a year on their writing, and of those, 30% spent more than double that. There's no reason you can't come up with something valuable to offer and grab a piece of that economy.

> **Take Action**
> How much money do you want to take home in your first year of book coaching? Write it down.

The Cost of Doing Business

As an entrepreneur working for yourself, you are going to have to cover the costs of doing business, which will include everything from taxes to health care, from paper clips to Post-It notes, from software licenses to internet access.

Taxes are dependent on a gazillion variable factors (e.g., where you live, how many kids you have, whether you have a home office, what your spouse does for a living, how you set up your business from a legal standpoint, etc.). I am not, therefore, going to give you advice on taxes. Not to mention that I can barely understand my own taxes. I pay a highly qualified professional who specializes in creative entrepreneurs to do my taxes, and I strongly suggest you do the same—and then factor that cost into your business expenses.

For the purposes of spitballing the cost of doing business, however, we need to factor in taxes. So let's say your tax rate is going to be 30%.

Example: You want to make $5,000, so you need to set your goal at $7,143 to cover your tax expenses. $5,000 is about 70% of $7,143, and the remaining $2,143 would be set aside for taxes.

Now let's add in some basic expenses a book coach will have. You'll have more than the ones I've listed, but one of the remarkable things about book coaching is how little overhead there is. You really could do this work with a laptop and an internet connection from your bedroom. So this list is representative of some of what you *might* need and what it *might* cost, but is, again, mostly a guesstimate. Your expenses will obviously be different.

ITEM	AMOUNT
A solid, stable, fast, computer (around $2,000)	
An internet connection (around $70/month or $840/year)	

Microsoft Word—The publishing industry runs in Word. One day it may flip over to software such as Scrivener but until it does, Word is the standard (around $130)	
Website hosting—I recommend Squarespace ($150/year)	
Email marketing software—Most platforms offer tiered packages based on the number of subscribers you have. Look for one that offers free services such as Mailchimp (free up to 2,000 subscribers)	
Office space—a home office will probably just cost you utilities; if you will rent an office space, this expense will be higher ($0 or rent + utilities)	
Video conferencing platform—Most platforms are free for calls with just one or two people ($0)	
Total Yearly Expenses	

PRO TIP: What expenses are tax-deductible for a book coach? This is an area I am not going to give specific advice in because I am not a tax expert, but according to *CoachTrainingWorld.com*, these are common tax-deductible expenses for a coaching business:

- Accounting fees
- Advertising (including website design and social media presence)
- Banking fees

- Business travel
- Computers and related tech equipment
- Consulting fees
- Education and training for employees
- Home office
- License fees
- Office supplies
- Rent
- Telephone service and equipment
- Utilities

Take Action
Take the "goal income plus taxes" number you calculated and add your expenses to it. This is what you need to earn per year in order to *take home* the amount you would like.

Play around with these numbers until you feel confident about the hours you can work, the expenses you have, and your total take-home yearly pay.

Using an Hourly Rate to Begin Setting Prices
We're going to use an hourly rate to do some calculations, but I *do not* recommend charging by an hourly rate.

Let me repeat that to make it crystal clear: *I do not recommend charging an hourly rate.*

Charging by the hour locks you into only being able to work a limited number of hours, and it's a game of hustle that does not value the knowledge you are bringing to your clients. You want your clients to pay for the *results* you are delivering, not how much time you are spending to deliver them.

At this point in my career, for example, I can read and evaluate a chapter in about 30 minutes, giving a clear and actionable summary of what is wrong and what needs to be done to get the chapter into pitchable shape. But would I charge half of an hourly fee for a chapter-evaluation service? Never.

Why? Because that thirty minutes could mean the difference between a writer landing an agent or not. Or attracting readers on Amazon or not. It is a very valuable service that I have honed over thirty years in the world of book publishing, and worth much more than the number of minutes it takes me.

I once bundled this service with a phone call and charged $1,500. I no longer actually offer these Instant Clarity Sessions for a variety of reasons I will explain later, but you can see that I did not base my fee on how long the work took me.

Despite the fact that I don't charge by the hour and don't recommend that you charge by the hour, for the moment, we are going to use an hourly rate to calculate your target yearly salary. It's the easiest way to understand the numbers.

You probably won't have forty hours of billable work each week, because you need to set time aside to work ON your business: to do marketing, sales, client onboarding and offboarding, invoicing, problem solving, networking, taxes, and the like. And you're going to get sick. And if you have kids, they are going to get sick.

So let's take a 40-hour work week and go back to our $18,000 side-hustle coach and our $60,000 all-in coach. Let's say that the $18,000 coach is going to work nine hours a week on coaching, and the $60,000 coach is going to work thirty hours a week on coaching.

Let's say these coaches are both going to work forty-five weeks a year, because one of the benefits of running your own business is that you get to take off time whenever you feel like it—and this is actually a topic worth talking about now that we are talking about hours and work.

At Author Accelerator, we don't work the last two weeks of the year. We also don't work the week of Thanksgiving. That means we are already down to forty-nine weeks of the year. I usually take two additional weeks off for vacations with my family. And I threw in an extra two weeks of time off just because.

A note, however, about time off and boundaries and a human-centered business: I find it really hard to shut business down completely. If I am on vacation and a client gets a phone call from a big agent and is blowing up my phone with celebration texts—"SHE SAID SHE LOVES IT!!!! I CAN HARDLY BREATHE! SHE WANTS TO REPRESENT ME!!! OMG CALL ME, CALL ME, CALL ME"—I will probably drop almost everything to take the call. If I am on vacation and a client gets a mega offer from a mega publisher in a mega auction, I will probably drop almost everything to celebrate with her.

I was once on vacation in a remote cabin with some other families, when I got a text that my client's feature story had been scheduled for the cover of the *New York Times* Sunday Review section. I'd helped him on the story and wanted to see it in the actual paper, not just online. So on Sunday morning I got in the car and schlepped into the little town and drove around until I found someplace that was selling *The New York Times*. It was a great moment.

It doesn't happen very often that a big moment in a client's career coincides with my time off, and when it does, I usually know it's coming and invite the client to contact me. I would find it horribly intrusive if a client randomly texted or called while I was on vacation.

Whatever your policy, you have to prepare your clients ahead of time and clearly set your expectations. That is part of the work of running your own business: knowing where you will draw the lines and boundaries, and knowing how much you care to work, and when.

OK, so to get back to the hours and our calculations about money.

In a year of forty-five weeks of working, the $18,000 coach is going to work 405 hours (9 hours/week). Divide $18,000 by 405 hours, and this coach is earning $44/hour for their coaching.

The $60,000 coach is going to work 1,350 hours (30 hours/week). Divide $60,000 by 1350 hours, and this coach is also earning $44/hour for their coaching.

> **Take Action**
> Play with these numbers—the total you want to earn, the hours you want to work, and the total dollars per hour that results in—until you are satisfied with the balance. Just get comfortable with the basic hours/total dollars equation.

We are going to use that hourly rate to start working on your packages and pricing.

Using an Hourly Rate to Think About Package Pricing

I said before you should never charge by the hour. That means there are two ways forward: to charge by the project or the page. I do a mix of both.

I charge by the project for almost everything except an evaluation or edit of existing pages. It's impossible to set a project price for those two things because a writer could turn in 50 pages or 500. I'll talk about those services in a moment.

With every other service I perform, I charge a project price. In the beginning of my book-coaching business, I would think about how long a certain project would take me, on average, as a way to begin to know what to charge. Take the review of a query letter. On average, it would take me about an hour to read the query and edit it. If I went on Amazon to look at comp titles and review an agent's website, went back to the edits and refined them, and then explained my notes to the client, you could call it another hour and a half. If the hourly rate I wanted to make was $44/hour, this would mean I would charge somewhere around $110 (2.5 hours of work) to review and edit a query letter. I might then round it up to $120.

There are two questions that proceed from this kind of an analysis. We'll use a query letter review as an example.

1. **Do I want to just get paid for my time?** As I said several times already, the answer is no. You do not. Because you only have a certain amount of time in the day, for one thing, and book coaching adds more value to a writer's work than how long it takes. When it comes to query letters, I know how a good pitch works, I know what red

flags to look for, I know how to spot a problematic writer-agent fit, I know how to research agents' wish lists, and I know how to optimize the book's hook to have the biggest impact. I am bringing a lot of value to the table—and I am bringing it at the point where a writer is desperate for help and the stakes are high. They are almost at the end. They can make a lot of mistakes at this stage and, with agents, mistakes are fatal. You can't go back to an agent who has rejected your work unless they ask. So the value of my contribution to a writer is also high. I would be short-changing myself if I charged $120 for this work.

What short-changing myself looks and feels like is that I would be constantly scrambling to find new clients in order to make more money, and constantly battling resentment that I was giving more to my clients than I was getting. It is a recipe for disappointment and burn out.

How much you might charge for each project depends on where you are in your career and what value you feel you can bring to the task. You might also consider the competition, which is a good indication of what the market will bear. But don't price yourself at the lowest end of the spectrum just because you are new to the work. If you can add value, you should be paid for it, and not just for your time.

2. **Does it do anyone any good to do a one-off review of a query?** Sometimes, in certain circumstances, it might. But I would argue that most of the time, it probably won't. A one-off read of a query letter does not take into consideration the writer's pain. What writers really need is for you to help them pitch with confidence; feel that they

gave their pitch the best shot so that, if they get rejected, they don't feel hopeless; and navigate the entire stressful situation with something other than panic. When considering pricing, you want to always think about the result the writer needs, the pain they need to resolve, and the transformation you want to inspire. That is where you bring your highest value. So bundling your query review with other services that will help the writer may be your best best.

I offer a pitch package, for example, that includes the following:

- Polish-editing of three sample chapters, which an agent might request
- Developing and polishing a synopsis and query letter with *as many rounds of feedback as needed* to get it perfect
- Developing a 30-name agent pitch list, which I will personally research and organize
- Coaching on how to rank the list (including how to deal with any friends of friends on the list, and any potential exclusive offer situations)
- Developing a strategy for pitching (How many to pitch at one time, in what order, and when.)
- Coaching on rejection letters that might come in (What do they mean? When should a write change their query?)
- Coaching on what to do when an agent calls
- Coaching on what to do when multiple agents call
- Coaching on the agent contract (with the caveat that I am not a lawyer and can only comment on whether or not the contract seems standard to me.)

I charge $3,500 minimum for this pitch package and peel off the coaching of the actual pitches and responses into an additional $1,500/month retainer.

The reason for the monthly retainer is that, almost without exception, when people are pitching, they will need to call suddenly because of some emergency. I have learned this. So in order to be able to make time in my schedule for those emergencies, I ask for the retainer. It's use-it-or-lose-it for them.

You can see that not charging by the hour is better for the writer, because even though it is more expensive they get better guidance and more thorough support. *They get what they need.* And it is better for me because I'm not doing a one-off ad hoc editing job that wouldn't be satisfying to the writer or to me. I get to deeply help the writer during a very difficult time and earn a solid income for doing it.

It is for this reason that I stopped doing the Instant Clarity Strategy Sessions at $1,500 that I mentioned before. People loved them, and I was selling an average of two to three per month, which was great, but I always felt sad doing them. I would solve a client's short-term problem and they would disappear. I didn't get to be part of the solution, and I found I really disliked that. I decided to stop offering any ad hoc services and only offer transformative services. This shift helped make my business stronger because it more clearly defines my value.

At the beginning of your coaching career, you just need to start doing work. You may well offer ad hoc services, you may not make much per job, and that's fine. It can work very well as you build a client base and confidence. Just keep paying attention to how things are working in your business, and don't be afraid to change over time.

You have to constantly recalibrate what you are offering, what you are charging, and how you are helping clients. Every six months take time to stand back and pay attention to what you love, to where your big successes come, to what people ask you to do over and over again. Knowing what you like best and where you can add the most value is the best marketing you can do. It also helps you manage client expectations, which is always a critical thing to do in an industry where you can't guarantee anything to anyone.

> **PRO TIP:** If you are feeling unsure about what to offer or skittish or nervous, just start with something. Go back to the nine business channels, find a pain point you think you can help with, put a fee on it, and start coaching. You will learn from the work itself about what clients need and what they value, and you will learn how you work and how long things take you. You don't have to get it right from the start. You can always change.

Take Action
In the next few sections you will define your service offerings and put a price on them. For now, play around with the numbers and write a bit about your thoughts on an hourly rate and ad hoc editing projects. What ad hoc projects might you start offering? What transformative services?

Setting Your Package and Your Prices
So how do you value your time and wisdom when you are starting your business? How do you determine what to charge?

Start by determining how long a task will take you—and *be honest*. This was an area I did not do well on in the beginning of my coaching career. I am a fast editor, so I tended to believe I was fast at handling client work, as well. I grossly underestimated how long things would take. I failed to consider that time on the phone cannot be sped up or slowed down. That handling invoicing and contract set-up takes time. That I might get interrupted. That things would go wrong.

I would suggest using a timer to time yourself on the tasks you want to undertake. Keep this data in a spreadsheet so you can be honest and clear with yourself.

One of the ways a book coach begins to earn more money is by getting more efficient at the tasks. In Author Accelerator's Advanced Book Coach Training course, we have several lessons on how to increase *editing* efficiency. Throughout this book, I will introduce some ideas for increasing *business* efficiencies.

RECOMMENDED READING

» Rachel Aaron's book *2,000 to 10,000* is about the writer's efforts to use data to increase her writing speed. It's a brilliant little book with much to teach anyone in the world of writing, editing, and coaching. Note that her intention is to increase her writing speed because that's how she will make more money.

Next, consider what your tasks mean to the writer. Remember their pain points and what they need at any given stage of the process. Try to name how you will actually be helping them beyond the edits on the page. This is to get your mindset out of the charge-per-hour game.

Examples:

- My work will help build their skill in writing scenes
- My work will help them slay their doubt about whether their writing is good enough
- My work will help them finally finish a book they have been unable to finish
- My work will help them finally start a book they have been unable to start
- My work will help them sort out a confusing part of the publishing process

Finally, consider your fears and limitations around the tasks. If you are new to book coaching and don't yet feel comfortable with the intensive pitch coaching, but you can certainly edit a query, synopsis, and a chapter, then just offer that until you can build your skills.

Consider, for example, a package with three rounds of edits on a query, synopsis, and first chapter priced around $550. Three rounds of edits means the writer will have very clear and solid pages they can feel good about sending out into the world. It's a value-added service to them and might take you in the neighborhood of ten hours. The last round of edits will likely be only minor mechanical tweaks, which would probably take a very short period of time, but again, would be very valuable for the writer. They will know their pitch materials don't have typos and that will give them confidence. You would earn in the neighborhood of $55/hour—and if the work came in clean and you became more efficient, you would earn even more.

This hints at a reality of setting your pricing by package: Sometimes you just lose the bet. Sometimes you get a client or a project that goes off the rails and, in order to serve the client, it takes you more time. That is the nature of the beast, and over time, it tends to even out. You can't fuss too much about it. You just do your good work, and as you increase your value to your clients, you can raise your prices.

Other packages you might offer include:

- Helping a writer define and structure their book at the very start of their project
- Helping a writer write forward and complete a draft
- Helping a writer plan and execute a revision of an existing manuscript
- Performing a Rejection Audit to determine why their work is being rejected by agents, editors, or readers
- Helping a nonfiction writer develop a book proposal, which includes information on audience, competition, and a marketing plan

Take Action

Develop two to three packages you intend to offer clients. Define the task in as much detail as you can to speak to your target clients and the value you are offering them. (If you're stalling out on anything related to page counts or per-page rates, leave them as TKs for now. TK is an editing mark meaning "to come." We'll get to those topics in a moment.) Then describe how many hours, on average, you expect the work to take you. Now set a price for each package.

PRO TIP: When you set a price for a package, deciding how to bill for it is a separate question. You could ask for the money all at once or ask for it over 3 or 6 or 12 monthly payments, or ask for it by a deadline (e.g., if the package includes deadlines, you could ask the writer to pay for each deadline as it occurs). I have landed on people either paying all upfront for packages, or in monthly installments. We are wired to pay for things monthly, so the latter option makes sense.

Projects by Page Rate

A package rate doesn't work for any coaching that involves evaluating or editing large chunks of pages. You might have packages that include one or two chapters, but when you're working on three chapters or more, or full manuscripts, you need to move to a per-page fee.

PRO TIP: The first thing you need to do when pricing by page is to make sure your clients are turning in standardized pages. In all my communications with clients, I request standard manuscript formatting, which is double-spaced 12-point Times New Roman font, with 1-inch margins on all sides and each chapter starting on a new page. This is the industry standard. If someone doesn't follow this standard, I make the change for them—once—and only edit the allowable number of pages. I then ask them to turn in the next set of pages with the proper formatting.

Manuscript Evaluations

The goal of this service is to let a client know how the book is holding together on every level—to evaluate it and give a thorough summary of what needs to be done. When doing an evaluation, you are not promising to make notes on the pages. It is important to let clients know it is not an edit. That being said, I actually do sometimes make notes on the page when I am doing a manuscript evaluation to point out what I am seeing and where. I have found this cuts down questions and also makes the writers feel that sense of delight I am going for—the sense that they got even more than they bargained for. You could also line edit a few pages and explain that this is a sample of what a full edit would look like.

When pricing an evaluation, you have to take into consideration how you intend to get through a long chunk of work. Do you want to set aside two or three full days to do it? Or do it over the course of several weeks?

I like to do all manuscript evaluations and edits over at least a month. This gives me time to read the work quickly and think about what I am seeing. I can study the marketplace, then read the pages slowly a second time and make my recommendations. I don't like being rushed on such a big project.

In my own coaching business, I charge $12/page for evaluations, which comes to $2,400 for a 200-page manuscript, but my price is set this high largely to dissuade people from asking me to do it, and so that if they do, I won't be resentful. I usually end up having to do manuscript evaluations at night or on weekends; my schedule doesn't have big chunks of time in it anymore, and for this reason, an evaluation can be very disruptive to me. If I am going to be disrupted, I want to be paid well for it.

I could, of course, just say no to all such jobs, and I often do. Someone who can't work weekends or doesn't want to work weekends, would need to carefully calibrate the time they have to do each job and make sure they leave enough time in their schedule to get the work done.

Obviously, for a big page count, my prices get astronomically high. I recently had someone ask me to do an evaluation for a 450-page manuscript. The total was going to be $5,400. When I did the calculation and saw that number, I had the instinct to lower it—because who would ever pay that? But then I remembered that *I* would have to pay in my time and attention, and that my time and attention were worth this price. I put a bid in to the client and he declined it because the price was too high. This was a good outcome for me.

When you are getting your business up and running, you will probably not charge that high a rate because you want those jobs and want to offer a reasonable price for them.

Manuscript Edits

The edit of a full manuscript is a demanding job, and a very valuable one for a client. Many writers write complete manuscripts that are riddled with problems and errors they can't see. They keep getting rejected in the marketplace because of it, and experience frustration and pain. By helping them identify their problems on both a global level (as an evaluation) and a specific level (as an edit), you are giving them a clear roadmap for success.

This work is generally called developmental editing.

The fee for this should be higher than your manuscript evaluation fee. At Author Accelerator, we charge $5/page for this work. In my business, I no longer agree to full manuscripts edits for anyone other than existing clients who have written their books with me. But when I did, I charged $15/page. I also used to do quite a lot of this work in the beginning of my career (for less than $15 a page, of course), and it's an important service a lot of writers need and value.

Copyediting and Proofreading

I don't offer copyediting and proofreading in my book-coaching practice. These are specialized skills I consider to be more a part of book production—the process that takes a manuscript from written pages to an actual book.

You can certainly offer these services in your business if you so choose. You might check the *Editorial Freelancers Association* or a marketplace like *Reedsy* to get a sense of what others are charging for these services.

> ### Take Action
> Set a per-page rate for any of your packages that are subject to variable page counts.

Zeroing in On Prices

At the beginning of your book-coaching career, you will want to set your prices at a rate at which people will accept them, but also need to make money, and you know what your time is worth. Finding the right price might take a while, which is fine. Don't be afraid to test your prices on actual clients, to see how you both react. Be aware of how you feel when you state a fee and the writer accepts it or rejects it; how you feel when you do a job and feel joy around it; and how you feel when you do a job and feel resentment around it. Tuning into these feelings is a way of gauging your own value and worth. If you constantly feel resentful about how much work you are doing for what you are getting paid, it's time to raise your fees! How you feel, more than anything else, should be your guide.

Studying the marketplace to know what other people are charging can be a great use of time when you're starting out, as well, so that you can get a good sense of the marketplace. I also recommend researching businesses outside of the book-coaching industry, since our industry is so new and so small. See what life coaches are charging, for example, or business coaches. I love signing up for other people's programs and services to see what it feels like to be on the receiving end of a sale, and to see how they are running their programs.

At the end of the day, research can only get you so far on pricing. You have to find a way to get comfortable with the money you are earning.

> **PRO TIP:** When doing your marketplace research, be sure to seek out a diverse pool of competitors. Research shows that women tend to charge less than men for the same work. In a *Medium.com* article entitled *Female creative freelancers charge 47% less than men. Who's to blame?* Abbey Woodcock presents a compelling case for setting high prices, but you need to balance that with the fact that you can't just open a new business, set high fees, and expect to attract clients. You may have to start low and build from there.

Giving Away Work for Free

The one thing I would caution never to do is give work away for free. There is one exception, which I will discuss in the marketing section of this book, but in general, *just say no* to working for free.

It deeply devalues the work you do, feels horrible, does nothing to promote you or your business, and I would even argue that it does little to help the customer. One of the reasons asking for help is powerful for writers—or anyone—is that it demands that they take *themselves* seriously. By contacting a professional, making a commitment, and putting money down, the writer is taking a huge step. If you make it too easy for them, they will not get the same result.

I have heard many healers—acupuncturists and chiropractors—explain that if people don't pay for their services, they won't heal as fast or even at all. As a consumer of a transformational service, you have to commit. You have to believe. And if it doesn't cost you, odds are good you're not going to get as much out of the relationship.

We found this to be true at Author Accelerator, as well. When we allowed people to come and go from our coaching program as they pleased, they did—and did not—finish their books or do their best work. People want to be held accountable. They want you to hold their feet to the fire. They want to *pay*.

Sales guru Kendrick Shope says that if clients are objecting to your fees, they are not actually saying they can't afford to pay the money. They are saying they can't afford to pay the money and *not have it work*. So your job is to convince them of your value, to earn their trust, and to be clear about how you can help them—not to lower your price.

Of course, if you need to start low on your pricing when you begin your business, that is fine. Everyone has to start somewhere, and building your confidence is critical. But start low with a plan for going higher. Put some measurements in place so you can evaluate your business plan and decide when to raise your rates to the point where you can make what you want to make.

> **PRO TIP:** There are a lot of ways to work for free besides straight-up working for free. Offering to do a sample edit for someone to show them how you work is working for free. (Instead, show them a sample you already have permission to share.) Offering a thirty-minute consultation call for a prospective client is working for free IF you begin to coach the writer on the call. If you keep it strictly to logistics and philosophy, then it's marketing. My problem is that I don't know how to NOT start coaching people, so the second I am on a call with someone, I am giving work away for free. I can actually solve a lot of problems in 15 minutes. So I have to check myself—or not offer calls.

Take Action

Write an addendum to your manifesto about when you will give away work for free and when you won't. Be specific. You are going to return to this manifesto whenever you are tempted, and you will be tempted.

Lowering Your Fees

I mentioned in the story about the 450-page manuscript that I considered lowering my fee for because I was sure the writer wouldn't pay it. It's fine to do this for the occasional project or person if you have a compelling external reason for wanting the job— i.e., it would be killer good for your marketing—but make sure you are very clear with yourself about why you are doing it:

- For the money?
- For the experience?
- For the testimonial?
- Because you love the person? (see next section)
- Because you love the project?

These are things you value that you might be getting from the project in addition to money, so lowering the fee might balance it out. But don't tell yourself a story about other people's ability or inability to pay, because you may have that story wrong.

Coaching Someone You Love

Loving a person does not mean that you should work for free or at a lower rate just because your sister or your neighbor or your writing group friends or a friend of a friend heard you're a book coach now. All these people will ask you about working for free—and it never ends. I have people ask *every week* if they can pick my brain or take me out to lunch to talk about their book or ask me a few questions about my thoughts on self-publishing. (Literally right now, I paused to check my inbox and there was a lovely note from a man whose wife is about to have a baby and they want to know how she might stay home to work as a book coach, and could I speak to them for an hour about how I've done it?) It's very sweet, but it never ends, and you have to take a very tough stand against it. Tougher than you probably want.

Here are some sample scripts for how you might respond to such a request:

- "I truly wish I could help every person who asks me for advice, but this is how I make my living…"
- "I am working hard to establish a business and have made a vow to myself not to…"
- "It is important for me to treat you the same way I would any other client, because I am concerned that if I do a favor for you on pricing, you will not value my work at the correct level."
- "I think it would be best for both of us to wait until you can afford my regular fees."
- "I think it is better that I not coach you, but let me introduce you to someone else who would be great…"

When I speak about taking a project because you love it, the love I am talking about has to do with *professional love*. Someone whose work you admire or who you are dying to work with or who would make an incredible connection or case study or testimonial for you. I have often done this in the name of marketing, but you want to be careful not to automatically offer a lower fee just because you love a project. It has to be love and for some excellent reason why the writer can't pay your fees.

I recently met a young professor at a writing conference. She was brilliant and dynamic and had a killer idea for a book. She understood the market inside and out, she understood the audience, she understood the competition, and she was eager and game and excited. I knew her book would be a commercially viable project. Her husband was still in school and there was no way they could afford my fee. I have nearly thirty book coaches working for Author Accelerator, so in these situations, I could easily hand off a writer to one of them, but I found myself not wanting to do that. I really wanted to work on this project with this writer. I offered her a fee that amounted to a 75% discount on my regular package price for developing a nonfiction book proposal. It was still enough money that it would be an investment and a commitment for the writer, and enough so that I wouldn't be resentful of the work. I also requested the right to use her material in future teaching situations, to which she agreed. We happily decided to work together.

> **PRO TIP:** In this scenario, the offer to work for a lower fee *came from me.* I doubt this writer would ever have asked me to do what I did. It was my offer, my choice, my initiative. I would be *very* wary of a client asking you for a reduced fee unless you have a pro-bono program or scholarship.

If you want to designate a certain number of pro-bono spots on your client list per quarter or year, you can certainly do that. These can be for people you want to honor with free services, such as veterans or people who have traditionally had a harder time getting heard in the publishing marketplace, or for young writers who may not have the funds to pay for coaching. But be intentional.

If you want to give one of these spots to someone you love, you might say, "I have three pro-bono spots open each year, and I would be delighted to give one to you, but I would like to ask you to go through my application and onboarding process so we can keep it professional."

> **Take Action**
> *Add to your manifesto some guidelines for when you might consider lowering your prices.*

Raising Your Prices

I know book coaches who have worked for many years and have never raised their rates. They have waiting lists and turn people away all the time and they still don't raise their rates. As your star rises, you can charge more for your work—and you should. It means your work is highly valued in the marketplace.

I want to take you through the progression I went through in my own business in terms of fees, so you can get a sense of my thinking at every stage. It may help you in your own work.

- **Hourly.** In the beginning of my business, I charged by the hour. I set my price around $50 an hour and thought that was pretty great! $50/hour seemed like a lot. I neglected to factor in the time I took to market my work, talk to potential clients, onboard them, bill them, deal with regular business issues like software upgrades and buying office supplies, and handle problematic clients. It turned out that $50/hour was not sustainable and didn't feel good.
- **Going from hourly to higher hourly.** I quickly upped my hourly rate, eventually getting to $120/hour. I thought this was the solution and was quite pleased

with myself. But the same thing kept happening where other expenses weren't being factored in, and, on top of that, I was WAY over-delivering, even at this higher price. The way I work with people is to go all in. I want my clients to achieve their goals and I want to do whatever I can to help them do that. I began to understand I needed to change my fee structure so that I could work the way I wanted to work.

- **Going from hourly to project rates.** I began to set prices by the package. This allowed me to work the way I liked to work, to deliver the kind of value I wanted to deliver, and to really help my clients meet their goals.
- **Going to higher project rates.** As my clients began to do well, I got more and more work—far more work than I would possibly be able to do. My solution for managing this problem was once again to raise my rates, thinking this would solve the problem of supply and demand. It didn't. I also learned that just because people can pay doesn't mean I want to work with them.
- **Going to an application-based in-taking process combined with higher project rates.** I added an application to my client in-taking process so that I could take some time to evaluate a project before I worked with the writer. If I chose not to work with them, or if they couldn't pay my fee, I would recommend them to other book coaches. It was around this time that I started earning six figures a year as a book coach.
- **Starting Author Accelerator.** I started Author Accelerator in part because I saw the opportunity to serve more clients by referring them to coaches whom I had hired and trained. When the company got off the

ground, I began to refer writers to Author Accelerator. We set our prices very low at first because I thought the market wanted lower-priced work.

- **Establishing longer required terms.** I began to require clients to work with me for a minimum of six months at even higher rates. Again, this allowed me to do my best work for the clients who were the best fit for what I was offering. This was also a big inflection point for my business; I earned *multiple* six figures as a book coach when I made this move.
- **Raising rates and terms at Author Accelerator.** Using the lessons I learned in my own work, we changed the way we work with writers at Author Accelerator, adding higher prices and longer terms of engagement.
- **In-person premium events.** In response to client requests, Author Accelerator added in-person workshops, so people can work directly with me, live. These are premium-priced events. The first one sold out, and we are planning more.
- **What's next?** My business has grown to a point where I work only by referral, and I have a waiting list. Clients must pay a deposit to hold a spot in my schedule, and I only take on a new client when one leaves, either because they are finished with their project or no longer need my services. As a result of this reality, my business coach has advised me to go to a long-term retainer model, meaning I would basically say, "I take eight clients a year at $30,000 each, by application only." Even though I am effectively doing this already, I have not yet been able to mentally make this leap and put it in these exact words. By the time you read this, I may have made the change.

PRO TIP: If someone is desperate to work with you and needs something done on a very fast deadline, don't be afraid to charge a rush rate. I did this for years, and it was shocking how often people needed it, and what they were willing to pay. I got to the point where I was charging double my normal rate if someone wanted something done very fast and refused to wait. I would only do this for clients I knew, or new clients whose projects were appropriate to what I was trying to do in my business. In one notable scenario, someone asked me to help them develop a book proposal in less than three weeks. She was heading off to a conference where she had signed up to pitch and had nothing to show. I asked if she was willing to work day and night, and to do whatever I told her to do, and to pay double my normal rate. She agreed. We did two months of work in less than three weeks, and she ended up getting a two-book deal.

You can see that it's been a work-in-progress the entire time. I constantly change how I work with clients, what I charge, what I offer, how I decide who to work with, and a hundred other variables.

Take Action
Make a note of when you think you might raise your rates. What milestone would you have to hit? What would trigger the increase in rates?

Total Clients Needed

How many clients do you need to serve to make your desired income? This, of course, depends on what kind of work you will be doing.

If you are helping writers with their query letter and pitches, they may not be paying you very much or staying with you for very long, so you may need far more clients than if you were helping writers evaluate and revise complete manuscripts. What you charge will also obviously factor into how many clients you work with. A book coach charging $5/page for edits is going to have to book more clients than one charging $15/page.

Take Action

Do the math with your business numbers and figure out how many clients you need across your variety of packages to hit your income goal.

You will return to this number each year to assess and evaluate what's working. They say that 80% of your income comes from 20% of your clients. You want to know who those 20% are and what packages they are buying, so that you can let go of the 80% that are not serving your needs.

In Part 4, we will work on how to manage the flow of clients and in Part 5, we will work on how to find the clients you need.

Setting Up Strong Business Processes

The more you can automate your business processes, the less time you will spend on each client and the more efficiently your business will run.

My business didn't become truly professional and efficient until I faced the fact that my business processes were a mess, and devoted time and resources into shoring them up. I did this by taking a course with Natasha Vorompiova at systemsrock.com and subsequently hiring her team to help me do a total overhaul.

Onboarding

Onboarding processes really begin when a client makes an inquiry about working with you, either landing on your website or contacting you directly. They will want to know your prices and your packages and will probably have many other questions about your coaching philosophy. The more you can streamline the way you present this information, the more efficient your business will be.

In Part 5, I'll talk about website development and how to present your business information online, but for this section, consider materials you can give to a potential client by email when they inquire about working with you.

FAQ and Rate Sheet

Every good business has an FAQ list. Some business FAQs are deeply entertaining and serve as an extension of the brand. Others are straightforward. However you present yours, you want to think through everything a client might ask about your business and present it in a professional way.

I use my FAQ when people first write to me to inquire about working with me. I send it along with a list of my packages and my prices so that people know what I do, what I *don't* do, how I work, and what I charge. Book coaching is a new gig, and many writers don't know what it is. I find I have to educate them. Having a FAQ document reduces the amount of time I need to spend answering these basic questions. Many clients look at these documents and decide they don't need to speak with me any further. This is a good outcome! It means that if they can't afford my fees or need something I don't offer or want a different kind of coach, neither of us waste our time determining if we are a good fit.

You can spend all day talking to people about your work rather than actually working. You want to preserve your time to do the work.

If you are just starting out and you don't have any work yet, offering a 30-minute phone call might be a smart way to gain confidence in speaking about your work, and discerning whether a client is a good fit or not. You can say the call is intended for you both to see if it's a good fit.

If, during the call, you decide you want to work with this person, feel free to say, "I would love to work with you, and I think I can really help."

If, during the call, you feel as though this writer is *not* someone you want to work with, you can say something like this:

- "My sense is that you are looking for a ghostwriter, not a book coach. I'm afraid I don't do that work. You could try looking _____ (with the blank being anything from "on Google" to the URL of a person or company you know)."
- "My sense is that you are looking for a guarantee about the outcome and that's not something I'm able to provide. I appreciate your inquiry, but I believe you would best be served by a different coach."
- "I don't actually have any openings at this time; since we set up this call, my schedule has filled up." (This may be a little white lie, but sometimes those are a saving grace.)

Take Action
Study other service providers' FAQs and notice how they make you feel—confident and eager to move forward, or stressed out and confused? Make a list of what you believe the FAQs for your business might be and begin to flesh them out.

Terms and Conditions

It is important to lay out the terms and conditions you will follow in your business. There is a tendency to be nice to people when they cancel appointments or miss them or send extra pages or forget to pay, and nice does not serve your business goals. Nice is going to make you feel like a doormat. I know this, because I have done it a million times. You bend for one client, then two, then three, and suddenly all you are doing is bending—and it hurts. And it's bad for business because now every single interaction or transaction is customized. Your ability to plan and streamline is shot. Your ability to plan your income is shot. It's not a good place to be.

You don't have to be a monster. If someone's mother dies and they miss a deadline, that is very different than if someone got busy and forgot to plan. But you want to write down the basic ways you intend to conduct business. You may or may not show these to clients, but they will inform your other business documents.

For Terms and Conditions, you want to think through the following:

- **Guarantees**—What exactly are you promising and not promising? You want to be crystal clear to avoid all confusion. What output can the client expect? What kinds of comments, what kind of summary, and what kind of assistance and guidance?

  PRO TIP: I do not guarantee that any project I work on will get an agent or a publisher or make the client money. I am very explicit that these things may NOT happen—and by explicit, I mean that I spell it out in my Terms and Conditions, in my contract, and in emails when I am going back and forth with potential clients. I bend over backwards to let people know there are no guarantees. We can't control a fickle marketplace. If someone has ANY problem with this whatsoever, I will not work with them.

- **Deposits**—Do you require them, and do you refund them? Under what circumstances?
- **Cancellations**—How will you handle clients who cancel deadlines close to the date, or who repeatedly cancel deadlines? What about emergency cancellations? What constitutes an emergency?
- **Payments**—How will you handle payments? Will you require deposits in advance? Will you invoice before the job starts or after the job is finished? See my notes in a few pages below in the section on taking payments.

Take Action
Sketch out the terms and conditions of your business practices.

Welcome Letter

When a client agrees to work with me, I first send a Welcome Letter to outline the basic tenets of the arrangement. This is a step that ensures we are on the same page about every aspect of the working relationship. I draw on my Terms and Conditions to formulate this letter.

As you consider this step, think about the following:

- **Expectations.** What do I expect in terms of my clients meeting deadlines, making payments, communicating, and other functions of the relationship? What can the client expect of me?

- **Technology.** What will I use to connect with my writers? Here, you want to think about how to share files and how to hold your phone calls and whether or not you will record them. Will you help your clients with technology they don't understand (with, perhaps, a video explaining it), or send them to the software provider to troubleshoot?
- **Next Steps.** I send links for clients to sign their contract, to pay their first fee, and to schedule their deadline calls on my calendar.
- **Communication.** I introduce clients to my assistant and discuss how people can reach her and when they can expect to hear back from her. You will probably not yet have an assistant, so clearly state your working hours and when clients can expect to hear from you. Should they call you on the phone if there is a problem? Text you? Email? When can they expect to hear back from you?

> ### Take Action
> Create a document you will use to welcome your clients.

Contract

I always have my clients sign an official contract. This too draws on the Terms and Conditions. I know book coaches who do not send contracts—and they have been burned. One coach I know had a client who became extremely successful, but her client refused to allow her to say they worked together; this is the kind of thing you can lock down in a contract. It may seem unnecessary or overkill, especially at the beginning of your career when you are perhaps doing smaller jobs for people you know, but it is important to get in the habit of putting things in writing, getting client's signatures, and level-setting the relationship at the start.

I also think this goes a long way toward helping the writer take the work seriously. If you sign a contract, and you put money down, you know that this is serious business.

The contract may overlap with the Welcome Letter, and that's fine. You can't state your practices too many times.

For your contract, think through the following:

- **Expectations and guarantees.** I repeat everything.
- **Work for hire.** I have a clause in my contract that says I make no claim on the rights to a client's story. I don't want there to be any confusion whatsoever, and I believe this gives my clients comfort.
- **Terms and conditions.** Once again, repeat everything.
- **Permission to use the client's name, likeness, and book cover.** Being able to talk about the clients you serve on your website and in your marketing materials is important to building a reputation. Make sure you lock down the right to talk about it.
- **Payment and cancellation policies.** Repeat, repeat, repeat.

PRO TIP: You may want to consider hiring a lawyer to go over your contract. I have had several lawyers and contract experts work with me on my contract over the years.

Online Contract Processing

I use an online contract processing vendor called Docusign. This system adds a small monthly fee to my expenses, but the ease of use and the official nature of the documents is well worth it. It lets your clients know that you are a professional and begins to build trust in your services and offerings.

> *Take Action*
> *Write a contract and decide how you will present it to your clients.*

Taking Payment

If you are going into business for yourself, you are going to be responsible for collecting payment. You want to ensure that you are not spending unnecessary time on this task—and believe me, you can spend a lot of time.

I used to have a terrible system—or, really, a lack of system—where every client had a different payment amount and paid me at a different time of the month, and some paid in advance of our working together and some paid after the work was done. People would pay by check, through PayPal, or through my FreshBooks accounting system via credit card. Every time I would work on a client project, I would have to figure out what they owed me, if they had paid me, and where they had paid me. I did not design it this way, but in the absence of a clear process, this is what emerged. It was stressful, upsetting, and caused me to have awkward conversations with clients (e.g., "Didn't you already pay me?" or "I thought you didn't pay last month?"). It was unprofessional and unsustainable.

When I overhauled the packages I offered, I overhauled the way I was paid, and designed a clean, clear, simple system that looks roughly like this:

1. Deposit is required to hold a spot on my calendar for future work. It's a hefty deposit and it is nonrefundable.
2. Payment is automatically taken by credit card each month via Stripe. I get permission to take the money out each month. I set up the recurring payment using a software called MoonClerk. Payment goes directly into my bank account. It is also recorded in FreshBooks, which is a small business accounting software I use to keep track of invoices and expenses.

If you are just setting up your business, you can take payment through PayPal or Stripe. It's easy and gives clients different options for how to pay. Just make sure you stick to one payment pathway, that you are consistent in when you invoice people, and that you have a way to easily track who has paid you.

I recommend having clients pay in advance of your doing any work. That way you're not chasing people down to try to get them to pay after the fact.

Take Action
Decide on a method for payment, and a method for invoicing your clients and keeping track of payments.

Scheduling

Scheduling clients can eat up a massive amount of your time. Writers are human, and humans get sick, go on vacation, have crises at work, have kids who need care, and have friends who visit. There are a lot of reasons for people to cancel deadlines or shift them around—and this can be bad for your business.

You want a steady and predictable stream of deadlines and income, and this means you need two things:

1. A scheduling philosophy to protect your time and income
2. A scheduling tool that puts the onus on the writer to set and change deadlines

Scheduling Philosophy

In the beginning of my business, I was incredibly flexible. I would allow writers to schedule deadlines whenever suited them—Mondays, Fridays, Wednesdays, whatever. I would also allow them to send in their work at any time on the stated deadline day, all the way up to the end of business that day. This meant that I had no way to predict who was sending what when, what I had to accomplish in a day, or when I had to get work back to clients. It was a hot mess and caused me a great deal of stress.

I finally got a grip and designed a scheduling philosophy. These are the main tenets:

- I design my workdays; I do not leave this up to my clients.
- I set the deadline date and time; I do not leave this up to my clients.
- Clients are not able to reschedule unless it is an emergency.

The result for me is a clean, smooth, systematized, and predictable schedule that looks like this:

- All writers with a deadline in a given week submit their work on Monday at 8 a.m. my time. If they do not submit at this time, they risk losing their deadline. I am very strict about this. No one ever misses their deadline.
- Each deadline comes with a client call, and all client calls happen on Thursdays and Fridays. There are only a certain number of slots on those days. Clients must book their calls in advance to ensure that they get the slot they want. I release deadlines and call spots three months in advance.
- If clients must change a deadline, they have to speak to my assistant.

I use Acuity to manage my scheduling. There are plenty of other powerful scheduling apps you can use, as well.

Take Action
Decide on a scheduling system.

Managing the Flow of Clients

As an entrepreneur you have to learn to manage the flow of clients, which means managing the constant tension between worrying about money and worrying about taking on too much work.

Determining how many clients to take on, and when to take on a new client, can become extremely complicated as your business grows. Unexpected things are always going to come up, such as a client having an emergency that demands they take a break, or a dream client coming along when you have no room in your schedule.

You have to get very, very honest about how much time and energy each client takes you and how many you can take on, and then you need a plan for what to do when you have to turn potential clients away.

Turning Clients Away

At every point of your business, you may need to turn mission-appropriate clients away—people who are right for your services, but whom you simply don't have time to serve. If you have determined you can serve just one client at a time and you get a second client who wishes to work with you, you have to turn that client away. If you have determined you can serve 12 clients and number 13 shows up, you have to turn that client away. What is the best way to do this?

Here are some options:

- Open and shut your application on your website with a simple landing page. If you are open to clients, they can contact you. If you are not open, give them a date when you expect to be and do not provide a way for them to contact you.

- Start a waiting list and let clients know when you expect your next slot to open up. Say something like: "My coaching slots are full at the moment, but I expect to have room next month. May I contact you at that time to see if you are still interested? You would be first on the waiting list." The waiting list can simply be a spreadsheet with clients' names and the date they inquired about working with you. When you have an open slot, you reach out to the first person on the list and see if they would like to sign up.

- Take a deposit so the writer can commit to that spot. Say to the client: "My coaching slots are full at the moment, but I expect to have room next month. Would you like to make a deposit to hold that spot?"

PRO TIP: I often give clients who have to wait for me something to do—a worksheet for an assignment I know they will have to do anyway, or a series of blog posts I wrote or a book to read. I sometimes customize this to their situation and pretend as if I am already coaching them. I have one package where, if writers commit to a future date and make a deposit, I send them a thirty-three-page Blueprint for a Book workbook that will be due on their first deadline. This makes it seem as if the delay in working with me is a planned and advantageous thing—and it often, in fact, works out that way.

Don't worry about turning clients away. Some will go on to work with other coaches, but others will wait for you, and, even if they don't, there will be more clients. Part of gaining confidence as a coach is knowing that the right clients will come to you and wait for you. This is much harder than it sounds. It's so easy to be frantic and take everyone who comes whenever they come, but that is not going to lead to a sustainable business.

Exceptions to the Waiting List

If you have no room for a new client and your dream client comes knocking, *must* you turn them away? The answer is: Of course not! I have often taken on a client when I absolutely could not take on a client, and I did so knowing that I would be working late at night and on the weekends to complete the work. It's fine to do this on occasion (if it works out with the people you live with) but just be intentional about your desire to do it, and honest about the cost to your well-being.

> **Take Action**
> Decide how many clients you will be able to take on and how you will handle a waiting list.

Offboarding Clients

It's important to know how to offboard a client. There are four different scenarios for how this might go:

1. **The writer achieves their goal.**

   They wanted to get a solid start on their book or finish a rough draft or pitch to agents, and they worked hard and achieved their goal. The first thing to do is remind them to celebrate! Seriously! Remind them that they did the thing they set out to do, and to take a moment to reflect and enjoy. Book writing is such a long and often difficult process that we have to urge our writers to mark the milestones along the way.

   The next thing to do is discuss whether there is anything more you can do to serve the writer, either yourself or by referring them to another professional. Sometimes writers want to take a break before they continue coaching, and it's a good idea to discuss what they want to do next and when, and to hopefully get it on your calendar.

I find that clients typically start asking about next steps far before they need it. When they start asking, I will often take time to walk a client through the process of what comes next and explain it to them. If I feel that our working relationship is good, I will indicate that I intend to see them all the way through until they reach their goal.

If your writer achieves their goal, you want to be sure to ask for a testimonial. In your contract, you will hopefully have already asked for permission to use the client and their work in your marketing, so this is a matter of asking for the actual words you can use. You may want to ask to use their photo, as well. Many times, writers will tell me wonderful and praiseworthy things in emails, thanking me for our work together. I write back and ask for permission to use those words on my website. You can leverage these testimonials in a variety of ways, which I will discuss in Part 5.

2. **The writer achieves their goal and the coaching relationship ends, but they keep asking questions, feedback, and advice.**
    This, unfortunately, happens a lot. It was a real problem for me before I got a handle on it. Clients tend to think that once they have paid to work with you, they get to have you on call forever. You need to make it clear to them that this is not the case.

The first thing is to consider having a "maintenance" phase of consulting. I do this with clients for periods when they know they will be busy with other things but still want to check in with me on various elements of their project. This often happens once a client sells or publishes their book. We might have regular calls less frequently than we were having before, and the expectation is that I will give them more general coaching about the publishing process or their book launch, and less of a focus on specific deliverables.

Another option is to offer ad hoc work. Make a list of services and pricing. How much would you charge if a client wanted you to edit an article based on their book that they have been invited to submit to a magazine? What about a speech? What if they would like you to review the edits the publisher's copyeditor did on their manuscript, or look over the cuts they made at the request of their editor? You will undoubtedly get such requests as your clients get farther in the publishing process, so it would behoove you to know whether you want to do this work, and if so, how you would offer it.

3. **The writer decides that they can no longer work with you because of money, time, interest, or energy.**
Writers are going to quit, so you should brace yourself for this happening, and build it into your income goals. Sometimes it is a matter of the writer feeling too much doubt about their project or too much pressure. Sometimes there are emergencies in their life or drastic changes to their budget. It is always a disappointment when a good client quits. You have put time and energy and

effort into helping them, and you are counting on them for income, and it doesn't feel good when they abruptly walk away. If circumstances are beyond their control, I always try to be as gracious as I can, and as generous as I can with the fees they may still owe me. I think this is good business, and it aligns with my business values. Sometimes the writer comes back later or writes later to say how much I've helped them.

If, however, someone just decides they don't want to write or don't want to work with me, I stick to the terms of the contract. This very rarely happens, since I am so careful about vetting clients when I onboard them.

PRO TIP: The work you did on your business values will serve you when you are dealing with clients who stop working with you. We had an unusual and horrible situation at Author Accelerator where a client died in the middle of a package she had paid for and committed to. The terms were clear that the money was ours to keep, but we immediately refunded the money to the family with our condolences and sent flowers as well. Terms and policies are only guidelines for your business. Your values should drive your behavior.

If you want to become an excellent book coach, you have to continually improve what you are doing. A growth mindset allows you to take in criticism from your writers and make constant improvements. If someone is not happy or seems frustrated, you want to ask why and how you might have prevented them from feeling this way. Even if the news doesn't feel good to hear in the moment, pleasing your customers is the single best way to grow your business. Disgruntled customers can also be pleased simply by being heard.

In the Advanced Book Coach Training course, I speak about how I manage giving negative feedback with compassion—it is the basis of my coaching practice. This sometimes means emailing a writer the next day when they are not on my schedule and asking how they are feeling after receiving the tough feedback. It might mean taking a little more time than usual to explain the next steps. It definitely means hearing them if they are angry or unhappy.

4. **You decide you can no longer work with a client. In effect, you fire them.**
A client who does not fit with your goals and your values and your superpowers is a bad client. The sooner you can determine the poor fit, the better. Ideally you do that during the intake process (also outlined in the Advanced Book Coach Training course), but it is not a foolproof method because it takes time to know who people really are.

Sometimes you are enthusiastic about a person and their project and then you get into it and they are not as they seemed. They constantly miss deadlines and make excuses or fight you on feedback. It's best to stop the relationship as soon as possible. It is not likely to get better.

I usually give someone I am concerned about two or three deadlines before taking any action, just to make sure my poor impression of them is borne out, and not to be too hasty. If things are not going well, I will say something like this:

- "I am feeling like the time is not right for you to be coached, or to be coached by me. You seem distracted or unable to commit to the work, which I completely understand. It happens. I'd like to suggest that we stop working together on this project. I can suggest another coach who may be in a better position to help you, or I can suggest a book or online class that may be useful to you."

- Here is a letter that an Author Accelerator coach wrote to a client. The two had worked together for some time before the writer took a break, and then came back with a whole new direction for the story:

  "I am attaching my comments on this week's pages. As you may suspect I have a lot of them this week! I know you mentioned that the changes you are making don't feel so big to you, but they do feel really big to me, and they are impacting your opening in challenging ways. You'll see all of my comments attached, but I wanted to say up front that I am finding the return to the story to be very difficult since we did so much work before that you are turning away from. That is 100% your right—as Jennie always says, you are the god of your story! But I fear that I am not in the best position, there-

fore, to guide you in this new direction. I think a new coach would be a much better support for you at this point. I want you to know that I am a huge fan of your writing and I have really loved working with you! This story is so layered and amazing, and your creativity is awesome, but I think a pair of 'fresh eyes' is really what's needed now. When you reached out initially I was under the impression that this was about 'tweaking' the ending and I wasn't quite pre-pared to take on this level of revision. Please let me know what questions you have—of course I'm happy to answer any of them! And please do stay in touch...I've really enjoyed getting to know you and would love to stay connected."

At Author Accelerator, we have a stable of coaches we can draw upon in these situations. If you are starting your own business, you may not have that at first. This is one argument for networking and meeting other coaches and forming a professional community. I will discuss this in greater detail in Part 5.

Once a project is finished, no matter the reason, archive that client's materials. Take a moment to review your systems and processes to see if there is anything you can improve that might help you avoid such a situation in the future. Take a moment to recharge before launching into something new.

Accounting

A few years ago, my husband and I set out to find a new accountant. We got recommendations from friends, asking people to give us names of accountants they knew who worked with small business owners, solopreneurs, and creative people.

We set up meetings and began interviewing people, and I was appalled at how every single one of them shook my husband's hand and not mine; and spoke to my husband, not me. I wanted to wave my arms and say, "YO! The business is MINE." Worse still, they acted as if my basic questions about some basic business realities were stupid.

We finally met a woman who worked with another woman in a casual office near the beach. She did not make me feel stupid for asking anything. She seemed sharp and on the ball. We hired her, and she has helped make me a better, smarter businessperson, and saved me a lot of grief and money.

This is what you should look for in an accountant. You can, obviously, do your own taxes if they are straightforward, but as your business grows, it is not likely to stay simple or straightforward.

An accountant can help you make decisions around:

- **Company structure.** One of the key questions an accountant can help you with is whether to open an LLC. There are pros and cons that I am not going to go into, because, again, it all depends on where you live and what your income is and what your family situation is. But it is a question you'll need to consider.
- **Savings.** Depending on your financial circumstances, you may want to plan for long-term savings. My accountant helped me decide to open an SEP IRA, which is a savings instrument for self-employed people, and I try to contribute the maximum each year.

- **Bank account and card.** You will likely want to open a business account with debit and credit cards attached, so that you can keep your business expenses separate from your personal. Your accountant can walk you through that process.
- **Taxes.** I mentioned taxes before, but it is worth noting that self-employed people must pay their own state and federal taxes on a quarterly basis based on what they are making. Having my accountant by my side has been enormously helpful in navigating the often-complicated process.

Filing/Organization/Backup/Processes

This is the part of the book where I get to talk about some of my worst failures. I am terrible at keeping my files organized and it has cost me dearly. I have spent more time than I would like to admit searching for material on my computer. I have multiple email addresses, multiple Google Drives, a whole universe in Dropbox, an inbox from hell, duplicated documents and folders, and, at one point, even a duplicated hard drive, taking up a huge amount of space (don't even ask how it came into existence...).

For years, I limped along, frustrated by this reality but embarrassed to ask for help in any capacity because I was ashamed to show anyone what the inside of my business really looked like. My advice to you is to set up an organizational system that will not embarrass or frustrate you—one that you will actually use—and then use it.

The one part of my system that works seamlessly is my client files, which are organized in this way:

- When a client signs up to work with me, I set up a shared Dropbox folder, with sub-folders for each deadline they have purchased. The subfolder has the number of the deadline (e.g., Deadline 1) and the date of the deadline, so there is no confusion. This is key!
- Each deadline folder has one subfolder for submissions and one for edits (which are named thusly). The writer uploads all their work to the Submissions folder. When I have completed my edits, they go in the Edits folder. This way there is no confusion. (Do you sense a theme here? When you are working with a lot of clients on a lot of projects, it's very easy to get confused.)
- When a writer has submitted their work on their deadline day, they email me to let me know the files are ready for review. I confirm with them that I have the files and that they are in my queue.
- I do two passes on all client work: On Monday, I do a quick read to get the lay of the land. On Tuesday, Wednesday, or Thursday, I do careful edits.
- When I have finished my review, I put the edited file in the Edits folder and alert the writer via email that they can look at the file.

No matter what organizational system you build, keep simplicity and clarity in mind. If you or your clients can't follow your system, it can be a huge drag on your productivity and ability to do your job well. Organization should not be the reason your business isn't succeeding.

Technology and Tools

There is always a new whiz bang technology to help you run a more efficient business, and it can be tempting to pile on a lot of software. Each one of those products is going to cost you money and take time to set up, so you want to carefully weigh just how effective it is going to be. The following is a list of the technology tools I currently use in my business—but keep in mind that my business is two-fold in that I am running a private book-coaching practice and also running a broader book-coaching business at Author Accelerator. You probably won't need all these tools at the start:

Financial

- FreshBooks—accounting software for small businesses; I organize my client invoices and expenses here, and track my income and tax payments
- MoonClerk—allows for recurring client payments via credit card
- PayPal—some clients prefer to pay with PayPal
- Stripe—credit card processing
- Venmo—instant cash transfers, which I sometimes use in a pinch

Productivity

- 1Password—I cannot live without this tool. It keeps track of all passwords and auto-fills them in on all online forms
- Acuity—calendar scheduling program; my clients get custom links to book their coaching slots
- Airtable—Author Accelerator's storage hub
- Asana—Author Accelerator's project management software. I know some coaches who manage clients within Asana
- Dropbox—I do all my client work in Dropbox so clients can see it and easily access it, and it is automatically backed up on the cloud
- Evernote—great for note-taking, keeping lists, compiling quotes and dozens of other tasks
- Google Drive—I store a lot of assets here that I use to send out to clients, such as sample query letters and proposals
- OneTab—I love this little tool. It's just a bookmarking tool but it's so much better than the browser one. I use this to store links to my Gmail, my calendar, my gym scheduler, my Asana tasks—all the daily tools I use.
- Toby—similar to OneTab but allows you to keep collections of websites; I often store things here to go back to read or watch or research

Communication

- ConvertKit—an email newsletter tool similar to Mailchimp but more robust
- Gmail—I use Gmail and a Google calendar, which I share with my assistant and my team

- Google Hangout—always good to have as a backup in case other forms of communication fail
- Loom—easily make videos of your desktop for training and sharing
- Mighty Networks—Author Accelerator uses this for our internal groups
- Skype—makes video calls easy
- Slack—instant messaging for my team
- UberConference—great for multiple people on a phone call
- Zoom—my preferred form of video conferencing and webinar hosting; it's easy to set up, record, run and download

Presentation
- Keynote—great for making slide presentations
- PowerPoint—I use this when a business partner prefers it
- Canva—easily make graphics for social media and other purposes

Website/Social Media
- Squarespace—I'm an evangelist for this website host. It's so easy to make clear and beautiful websites
- Bitly—instantly makes tiny URLs for use on social media

Audio
- Bose noise cancelling headphones—shuts the world out, makes phone calls clearer

- Technica microphone—a gift from my podcast PR professional; before I had this one, I used the Yeti microphone.

Physical Comfort
- Herman Miller Embody Task chair—enormously expensive but I love it
- Apple Thunderbolt screen—makes documents giant
- Apple Magic trackpad and Bluetooth keyboard—makes working at the giant screen easier

When Should You Quit Your Day Job?

This is obviously a highly personal matter that, like taxes, must take into consideration your total family income, your dependents, and your cost of living, as well as how you are doing in your business compared with your projected goals.

No matter when you decide to take the leap, it's going to be a leap of faith. You're going to have to trust your ability to make a sustainable living.

You may also want to consider the general health of the economy—although I have found that the demand for my services does not seem to fluctuate with the economy. It means that the clients I serve have the ability to pay for book coaching regardless of the general health of the economy. If anything, I often see an uptick in work when the economy is bad; people who have lost their jobs or lost a lot of money sometimes reflect on what is really important to them, and what brings meaning to their lives, and decide that writing a book is more valuable to them than they previously believed.

A big roadblock for many people in quitting their day job is health insurance. Similar again to taxes, I can't pretend to know how to advise anyone on this topic, and it is a topic that seems to always be a moving target as the laws and options change. There is a good *Inc.* article on health insurance by Heather Wilde at jennienash.com/readbooksallday.

PART 5

Marketing Your Coaching Business

There are a gazillion great books on marketing—some of which I recommend a few pages below—and it would be impossible to outline everything you might need to know about marketing your book-coaching business. It will be a lifetime learning process for you, just like it has been for me. Running a good business is about trying and failing, studying and tweaking, pivoting and optimizing, over and over and over again, and there is no substitute for that work.

The secret, I think, is realizing that *no one knows what they are doing.* No one knows what works. I make multiple six figures as a book coach and run a half-million dollar plus book-coaching company and I can't tell you what, exactly, works when it comes to marketing.

I can say that having a clear sense of purpose works and having integrity works and delighting customers works. But have the specific ads I've run on writing sites or in writing magazines worked? Have the guest posts I've written, the podcasts I've been on, the conferences I've presented at worked? It has all depended on myriad other factors. There is no one thing you *must* do that will be *guaranteed* to work.

Marketing success is made up of a constellation of factors, and the main thing is to just keep trying—listening to your customers, serving them, and paying attention to what they are asking for. There is no magic bullet and anyone who tells you otherwise is not, in my mind, being fair or honest about the realities of business.

All this said, there is a huge benefit to seeing what others have done, so I will attempt to share with you some things I have learned about marketing a book-coaching business, in hopes that it will help you kickstart your own business.

First Off, What NOT to Do

- Don't join marketplaces of freelancers (such as *Upwork* and *99Designs*) that promote a race to the bottom on pricing. You will end up charging less than you are worth, taking jobs that don't advance your career, and feeling resentful. It's not worth it.
- Don't give away work for free unless it's part of a very strategic launch plan (which I will outline).
- Don't spend a ton of money on a website designer or a logo or any of the bells and whistles of how your business looks. You want a professional presentation to be sure, but anything beyond that is frosting on the cake. You need to bake the cake first (i.e., build your business). I still don't have the website of my dreams, and it is not hurting my success.
- Don't fall into a scarcity mindset and convince yourself that there isn't enough work for everyone. There are enough writers for everyone. Having a scarcity mindset—the idea that if you succeed, it means I won't—isn't true, isn't helpful, and I think it can actu-

ally do you harm. Book coaching is a new industry. We are still developing and still growing, and all of this is in response to demand. There is a lot of demand! I believe that if we help each other and lift each other up, it lifts all of us up.

Understand the Publishing Marketplace

We have spoken in these pages about the marketplace of writers—the universe of people who want to write and publish books. You know their pain points and the main channels where they do business. I believe you need to keep your antennae up about this universe—how it is changing and moving and growing—so you can continue to refine your place in it.

Find good sources of publishing business news and read them consistently. Continue to educate yourself about the world you are working in. Some of my favorite sources about publishing news include:

- *Shelf Awareness*—a newsletter for booksellers that is one of the best places to learn about what is happening in publishing
- *Publishers Marketplace*—where deals are announced
- *Manuscript Wish List*—the best way to keep a pulse on agents who are open to submissions, and on what the trends are. Agents might say things like, "Please don't send me any more #MeToo memoirs," and you can be sure that the marketplace has been flooded with those kinds of books.
- *Twitter*—There are so many writers and agents on Twitter. If you feel nervous about Twitter or scared of

it, don't be. Get a handle, get on there, follow me, follow anyone you know and admire in publishing, and just start watching the commentary. When you feel comfortable, start commenting—start with tiny, positive things, like, "So interesting," or "I agree," or "Can't wait to read that book." Then work on optimizing your profile, sharing interesting posts of your own, making more in-depth comments, and identifying who the big players are.

- Jane Friedman's newsletters, both her regular one and the one called *Electric Speed*, which focuses on technology and other tools. She is just so smart about publishing trends and so well connected that you can learn a ton by following her.

- Genre-specific organizations such as *Society of Children's Book Writers and Illustrators, Romance Writers Association,* and *Thrillerfest*.

- Podcasts. There are hundreds of podcasts about the craft of writing and the art of reading, and many hundreds more about creativity and productivity, and more still about entrepreneurship. Google top podcasts, listen to some episodes, and find the ones that speak to what you are doing.

Take Action
Sign up for three industry newsletters, blogs, or sources that you feel will be most helpful to the business you intend to run.

Understand the General Principles of Business

You don't need to get an MBA, but I do think it is advantageous to educate yourself about how business works in general, and especially how a freelancer service business works, since that is what coaching is.

A lot of coaching businesses don't thrive because the coach doesn't understand how to identify their customers, how to find them, how to convince them to pay the prices they need to charge, how to delight them, and how to get them to come back and refer the coach to their friends.

Seth Godin, the guru of permission marketing, describes freelance business this way:

> *"Figure out how to do the best work in your field, the best work for the right clients. Don't fret about turning away work, and don't fret about occasional downtime. You're a freelance for hire, and you need to focus on your reputation and the flow of business... Freelancers get ahead by becoming more in demand, by charging more (and being worth it). They get ahead by being more connected, smarter, more effective."*

The key questions for your business then become: How do I get connected? How do I get smarter? How do I get more effective?

None of this can be achieved by taking out an ad. You need to focus on delighting your customer, delivering huge value for what you are charging, and networking with other people in the industry who can help you do your best work.

RECOMMENDED READING

» Jane Friedman's book *The Business of Being a Writer* is an excellent resource for understanding the *writer's* side of the business, which will help you become a better book coach and run a better business.

» You can learn more about Seth Godin's marketing philosophy in his book *This Is Marketing*, which is enormously informative. I am a fan of all of Godin's other books, as well.

» I also like *Marketing: A Love Story* by Bernadette Jiwa and *Anything You Want* by Derek Sivers.

RECOMMENDED RESOURCES

» There are so many amazing podcasts about starting a business. I find them instructive and inspiring! I love *Mixergy*, for example, and *She Did It Her Way*, and the *Being Boss* ladies.

» There are also hundreds of great courses and communities to learn more about business. We have a community of book coaches at Author Accelerator, for example, which you can join through our Book Coach Training and Certification Program. Tara McMullin runs a robust and effective community of small business owners in her *What Works Network*. There is also the *Female Entrepreneurs Association*, which is big and sprawling but also fun.

Get Your Messaging Right

I believe that getting your messaging right is one of the most effective marketing tools you have to work with. When someone asks, "What do you do?" You need to know how to answer. When someone lands on your website, it needs to be crystal clear what you offer, who you work with, and what outcome you are promising.

The biggest mistake people make in this regard is trying to serve everyone. (This is also, by the way, one of the biggest mistakes writers make.) This is usually a decision made out of fear—fear that if you turn away one client you will never get another. I get this fear. I have lived with it for as long as I have worked for myself. I used to fret about my next job and my next client all the time, until my husband began to say, "When was the last time you didn't have enough work?" The answer is, more than twenty years ago. I was worrying for no discernable reason. All I had to do was keep doing what I was doing, keep delighting my customers, and keep talking about my work in a consistent and compelling manner.

How will you talk about your work? What words will you use to describe what you do?

Pia Silva is a brand consultant who writes a *Forbes* column for small business owners. She says:

> *"If you're wondering why you're having a hard time coming up with that show-stopping brand message (you know, the one that perks up people's ears and makes them beg to hear more), then you should probably go back a step and consider where your business's best opportunities are and if you are willing to narrow to grow and expand. Stop trying to be everything to everyone."*

Bernadette Jiwa, marketing guru and author of *Marketing: A Love Story* and *Story Driven*, echoes this concept:

> *"Every one of us — regardless of where we were born, how we were brought up, how many setbacks we've endured or privileges we've been afforded — has been conditioned to compete to win. Ironically, the people who create fulfilling lives and careers — the ones we respect, admire and try to emulate — choose an alternative path to success. They have a powerful sense of identity. They don't worry about differentiating themselves from the competition or obsess about telling the right story. They tell the real story instead. Successful organisations and the people who create, build and lead them don't feel the need to compete, because they know who they are and they're not afraid to show us."*

You have to choose. You have to put a stake in the ground. The simple act of claiming this kind of authority—of knowing yourself and your superpowers—will attract the customers you want. I am not talking about the law of attraction here, although if you believe in that and it works for you, all the better. I am talking about clarity and intention and confidence and authority. These are things that get people's attention, especially when combined with stellar work.

Take Action

Develop some messaging about the benefits of working with you. What makes you awesome at what you do? What are your superpowers? Why should someone hire you? What will they get out of it? What exactly are you offering?

Use your mission statement and your packages to guide you. Remember the audience you decided to serve. Think about what you want your writers to walk away knowing or doing or having accomplished.

This is your moment to brag. No one has to see your drafts. You can go big as you brainstorm and if you feel uncomfortable, dial it back when it comes time to put the words on your website or say them out loud.

Once you get your answers on paper, you can begin to refine the messaging for your website.

If you can't clearly define what you are doing and why are you are great at it, go back and refine those elements until you can.

It can help at this stage to go back to the competitors you studied in Part 2 and review their messaging. Is it clear who they are serving? What services are they offering? Why might someone choose to work with them instead of you? Make it easy for people to choose you.

RECOMMENDED RESOURCES

» Brand expert Pia Silva's columns on ***Forbes.com*** about messaging and how to reach your audience are great learning tools for this step in the process.

» Everything at ***Copyhackers*** is also enormously useful. They A/B test headlines (which is a comparative analysis to see what is most effective), give you swipe lists of effective messages—all the data, in other words, behind what works and what doesn't when it comes to website messaging. Beware that this site might suck you in for days. (And note how *generous* they are with their data and knowledge—something we will talk about in a moment.)

» Bernadette Jiwa's ***Story Driven***.

Develop a Professional Website

A professional website that clearly states your services and reflects your values and speaks to your audience will be the foundation of your marketing outreach. It doesn't have to be fancy; it just has to be effective at conveying your message.

The key decision is: What action do I want my potential customer to take when they land on my site? What do I want them to *do*? The possibilities might include:

- Sign up for a blog or newsletter
- Download a giveaway—a short course or video series or infographic
- Attend a live event or webinar
- Sign up for a consultation
- Purchase a service

Your answer may change over time. You may run a promotion and then decide to end it. You may want to try a variety of approaches to see what works. You want to be flexible and nimble—to pay attention to your customers' needs. For example, my website had a very expensive service offering on the home page for a while. This was by design. I was not looking for new clients. My goal, in fact, was to dissuade people from reaching out to me. I wanted a way to showcase what I do, frame myself as a high-priced coach, and turn people away who were not a good fit. This worked very effectively—until it didn't. Too many people took advantage of the offer.

This need for flexibility argues for being in control of your own website, not farming it out to a designer. I love Squarespace. You can make a professional website using their templates for about $250 a year. They have a library of tutorials to teach you how to do almost anything, and amazing customer service for when you get stuck.

> **PRO TIP:** Do you need a fancy logo? At the beginning of your business, I don't think so. Squarespace has a function where you can make a logo with some simple fonts and design elements. You can also do this with other free or low-cost logo-making sites or software, some of which allow you to pick a style and work with a designer to make it your own. You can also, of course, go out and spend a fortune on a logo, but I don't think it's necessary. Get your website in good shape, focus on your messaging, and wait until your business is cooking before you add the bells and whistles.

None of what I am saying here is meant to knock website and graphic designers. I love graphic designers! Their skills are incredible! But you can easily spend $3,000 or $5,000, or more, for someone to design a site that you can't change without going back to them. There is a time and a place for that—but I don't think it's at the beginning of your business.

Necessary Website Elements

- You need a way for your clients to pay you. As I mentioned before, PayPal is an easy place to start. You can set up direct-pay buttons right on your site to take money for your packages.
- You need a way for your clients to contact you—an email address or contact form. This evolved for me over time, as well. I used to be very open and welcoming. I would talk or email with anyone. It gave me a way to learn what people wanted or were looking for in a book coach. I then evolved to a place where I had a very complex intake Q&A right on my site. This was designed to weed out the looky-loos—to attract people who were serious about working with me. It worked.
- You definitely want testimonials on your website to give potential customers comfort that you can deliver what you promise. Chris Guillebeau, author of *The $100 Startup*, says you should have "at least two stories of how others have been helped by the service (if you don't have paying clients yet, do the work for free with someone you know)." I'll explain how to get those testimonials in the next section on creating a business launch.

PRO TIP: When your business starts cooking and you begin to get some wins—clients who achieve their goals, who feel deeply pleased with their accomplishments, or who sell books, land agents, and get book deals—you want to be sure to find a way to trumpet those successes on your website, in social media, and as case studies. Nothing builds your reputation like success stories—and remember, success does not have to mean Big 5 book deals. Success is your clients achieving their goals. Try to get them to write something or better yet, record a video about how your services helped them.

- Professional bio and photo. These are not throw-away elements. This is part of your branding and messaging and gives people a way to get to know you and trust you. As part of his human-centered marketing programs at wegrowmedia.com, my friend Dan Blank begins by teaching people how to write their professional bio in a way that is authentic and effective—it's that important.
- Every small business expert will tell you that a newsletter that allows you to directly contact your audience is the No. 1 business asset you want to nurture and develop. It's where you can be generous and authentic and put a stake in the ground for who you are, what you believe, and what you do. I will discuss newsletters in more detail in the *Find a Way to Connect* section. For now, here's what Tim Grahl, author of *Your First 1,000 Copies*, and book launch expert, says about

email lists. He is speaking here to authors but what he says is also 100% true for book coaches:

"Myth #3: I don't need an email list. *This is usually where an author lists off some famous or semi-famous author and how successful they are and they don't have an email list so why do I need one?*

So let's start with the famous authors.

If your name is Nora Roberts or Stephen King or John Grisham, you don't need any email list. The publisher has paid you some enormous advance and they are going to put you in every bookstore and run every promotion and advertisement they can to get the book out into the world. Not to mention the millions of fans the author has already built up over decades of writing.

However, if you're not one of those authors, you need some way to notify your potential and current fans that you have a new book coming out when it's time to launch.

How do you plan on doing this without an email list?

You can buy advertising, but it's expensive and unpredictable. Also, you'll find that over time you have to pay more money for fewer and fewer results.

There is social media, but it is extremely unreliable and does not sell books well.

Right now, if you look out at the digital landscape, the tool that will sell your book the best is an email list.

Do you have to have one? Of course not.

I don't have to have a lawn mower to cut my grass. I have a perfectly good pair of scissors that will cut the grass just fine. I would just be opting for an extremely inefficient way of going about the job.

You don't have to use email marketing for authors.

You can go with buying advertising or building a Facebook page or getting more Twitter and Instagram followers. Just know you're going about it in a less efficient way."

Should You Combine Your Writer's Website with Your Book Coaching Website?

Many book coaches are writers or are in the midst of building their writing career, and if that's you, you may already have a website dedicated to your writing. So does it make sense to build a new one for your coaching, or to combine them? There are obviously pros and cons to every decision, but until your book-coaching business becomes a full-time job, I don't think you need the expense and hassle of having two sites.

Your writing can be a way to help sell your coaching and vice versa. There is a lot of synergy between the two businesses and it makes some sense to combine them into one whole—until, as I said, it doesn't.

I asked Dan Blank about this element of marketing for book coaches. This is what he said:

"Go all-in on forging a single identity as someone obsessed with writing. Illustrate how you do that for your own books and shorter pieces, and how you then help others do the same. Your online presence should

make it obvious that you walk the talk, and the two sides should make each other stronger. You want to show that you study the craft of writing in order to help your private book-coaching clients, as well as create your own books."

Take Action

Make a map for your website. What navigation tabs do you need at the top? What main action do you want people to take? How will your messaging flow through your site?

Connect with People

Marketing a book-coaching business is not the same as marketing Coca-Cola or Tide detergent. You can't just take out a billboard or an ad in *Writer's Digest* and start attracting clients. You need to connect with people in an authentic way. You need to build trust in a personal, meaningful way. Typically, this is going to happen one person at a time. I realize this is not as exciting or inspiring as giving you some solution where you can instantly get 5,000 followers, but it's what I know to be true.

There are several ways to do this work:

1. **Connect with people by sending out a newsletter or blog.** As I mentioned, this is the best way to build an audience because people who opt into your newsletter have given you permission to market to them. You don't want to be selling all the time, however—not by a long shot. You want to be generous and helpful and respond to what people most need from you. This means you need

to have a clear sense of who you are speaking to, write compelling content that will actually help them, and be consistent about when you send it out. You might share your knowledge, help writers with their pain, or help them understand what is happening in publishing.

> **PRO TIP:** You can start a newsletter right on your website with a platform like Squarespace. You can use *Mailchimp*, which is cheap and easy to use, or a similar email marketing software. Later, if you start running courses and workshops and need to slice and dice your list, you might consider a more robust system like *ConvertKit*, which we use at Author Accelerator.

2. **Connect with people on social media.** People tend to think that social media is totally overwhelming, but it doesn't have to be. If you are intentional about what your goals are, intentional about how and when you use it, and intentional about which platforms you spend time on and who you follow, it can be an incredibly effective way to connect with potential customers. Here are a few things I have learned about social media as a business owner:

    - Limit the time you spend on it. It's so easy to get sucked in. Obvious, but it bears repeating.
    ◦ Follow influencers—other book coaches, writers, and experts in the field.
    ◦ Be a good literary citizen. Write Amazon reviews for the authors you read, retweet people's posts if

you think your audience will appreciate them and thank people for doing the same for you. There is room for everyone in the publishing universe, and I believe we should work on lifting each other up.

∘ Spread the love. Be kind and generous and helpful. Respond in a positive and authentic way to influencers you admire, potential colleagues, authors, and those trying to learn their craft. Generosity is a good business practice. It is something I have tried to practice in every realm of my work life and is directly connected to the value I have of wanting to delight my clients. I want them to be super pleased with my work. I want them to rave about me to their friends. As a result, I am as generous as I can possibly be with my time and my attention and my wisdom—not just for my clients but for my newsletter readers and for the people in my workshops and people I meet on social media and other book coaches. I think it is effective and it also feels like the right thing to do.

RECOMMENDED RESOURCES

» Once your business picks up steam, you may want to consider spending money on ads. These generally work well for events or webinars, and there is a science to doing them—and to keeping up with the constant changes in policies and best practices. There are dozens of great ways to learn about optimizing social media. I recommend Amy Porterfield's courses and Mark Dawson's *Advertising for Authors*. Yes, it's for authors, but you will learn the skills you need, as well.

» Dan Blank's *Be the Gateway* is a fantastic book about what human-centered marketing looks like. He demystifies many of the things about social media and marketing in general that terrify people.

- **Connect with people in person.** Don't underestimate the power of the old-fashioned face-to-face meeting or 1:1 time with another person that has no other benefit other than connection. Almost all of the successful business people I know do this, in one form or another. Here are some examples of how this looks in my business:
  - I meet once a week with Dan Blank. We spend 30 minutes talking about a business challenge he has and thirty minutes talking about one I have. We have been doing this for five years. We met on Twitter when we each started retweeting the other's work.

- ° I recently moved to a new town and began connecting with writers and other creative entrepreneurs. I reached out to friends of friends and even met people on Twitter for in-person blind coffee "entrepreneur" dates. I met some incredible people this way. Yes, it's awkward to make the ask, and it's sometimes awkward to do the meetup, but the payoff can be amazing. You will feel connected to a web of people who are doing similar work.

- ° Whenever I attend a conference or workshop, I look for colleagues to connect with. I go out of my way to track them down and say hello. I tell them that I admire their work. I ask if we might set up a time to chat in person at the conference or afterward by phone. And I follow through. I recently had a phone call with a woman I met at a conference. We literally had a three-minute conversation at the conference, but it was a great conversation. We agreed to talk on the phone once we both got home. We set a time, and I had to cancel. We set a time, and she had to cancel. We finally had the chance to chat and it was lively and fun and productive—the best part of having gone to the conference. A byproduct of our interaction is that we came up with a fun thing to do together that will enhance both our businesses.

Take Action
Make a list of ten people you would like to try to connect with about your business. Indicate where you think you can best connect with them.

Make a Business Launch Plan

If you are just starting your book-coaching business, you have the opportunity to launch it—to make a big splashy entrance into the marketplace. You can also do this even if you've been in business for a while, by launching a new package or a new website.

Big and splashy is, of course, relative. I am not talking here about going viral or trending on Twitter. This is what I have in mind:

1. **Secure at least three testimonials for your website.** If you have to give away work in the beginning to get these testimonials, that is so fine! It's very smart! You might put out a request to your writer friends or on social media. Be extremely clear. You might say:

   "I am looking for three beta-test clients to try out my new book-coaching services. I will be offering 50-page edits of YA novels-in-progress in exchange for a testimonial I can use on my website. I will want to use your name and your author photo. Please apply by emailing me to let me know you are interested. I will send you a new client Q&A and we will go from there."

2. **Update your website and all your client in-taking processes** and have them ready to go. Be sure to have a place for people to sign up for your newsletter. You want their names and email addresses. You want to be able to reach out to them directly!

3. **Consider some kind of fun giveaway** for your launch or a fun event that will attract people to take a look at what you are up to. This can be anything from a free webinar to a free download to an internet treasure hunt.

4. **Tell everyone you know that you are open for business.** Tell friends, family, co-workers, neighbors, and people you are connected with on social media. Do this in a strategic way with an announcement on a certain day, and coordinated digital communication (e.g., an email to your newsletter list and social media posts). Work backward from this date to plan out the other elements you need to have in place for the launch.

5. **Get business cards** and carry them with you at all times. Whenever anyone asks what you are up to or what you are doing these days, tell them about your book-coaching business and give them a card. Practice saying, "I recently opened a book-coaching business." They will ask what that is, and this is your chance to give a version of your mission statement.

RECOMMENDED RESOURCES

» Jenny Blake, business consultant and author of the book *Pivot*, has an amazing array of templates you can use to launch a business, and she gives them all away for free at *PivotMethod.com*. She has one for launching a website, which you can adapt to your business launch.

» Paul Jarvis, author of *Company of One*, a great book about working for yourself, has a complete checklist of everything he did for his book launch at pjrvs. com/launch— and his was a *very* comprehensive launch plan. It's obviously about a book launch, but many of the steps are exactly what you need to do to launch a business.

» Tim Grahl's book, *Your First 1,000 Copies*, gives a simple, systematic way to launch a book. His advice is very relevant for launching a book-coaching business, as well.

» I run a mentoring program to help book coaches through the steps in this book. You can learn more at jennienash.com/readbooksallday.

Take Action

Make a launch plan for your business, listing out every action you need to take, and a date for when you will launch

PART 6
....

Writing a Business Plan—
Putting It All Together

N ow that we have touched on all aspects of your business, it's time to put together a Book Coach Business Plan. I am a big fan of reducing things down to a couple of pages because it forces you to be concise and intentional, so aim for no more than three pages. This allows you to look at the whole sweep of your business in one glance, which makes it far less overwhelming. And you can easily share the plan with trusted friends and advisors to get feedback.

If you find yourself thinking that it's impossible to put this all on a few pages—think again. You can absolutely do it and doing so forces you to focus and get specific, which is the key.

> *Take Action*
> *Download the Book Coach Business Plan template at jennie-nash.com/readbooksallday*

PART 7

Optimizing Your Business

If you are just starting your book-coaching business, you are probably only thinking of hitting your client numbers, getting your business's processes in place, and making it *work*—but at a certain point which might not be that far in the future, you may find yourself in a position to take your business to the next level. To do this, you may want to revisit the 9 business channels we mentioned at the start and think of ways to move into other channels.

Here are some of the ways you might consider doing that.

Creating a Sales Funnel

A sales funnel is a series of offerings to draw people into your universe and introduce them to your services. It's called a funnel because the offerings typically get increasingly more expensive as you add depth and lead customers to your core service. Some coaches give away a PDF or an infographic at the top of the funnel, as a fun introduction to their work. This product is designed to appeal to a broad number of people and is usually free. It might then lead to a webinar or a series of emails about a given topic that offer more information and may require the customer to pay a fee or sign up for an email list that the coach can then use to market their core service to those customers.

Once you become known for a particular service, you might consider creating a longer course on a platform like *Teachable* or *Udemy*. My courses on *CreativeLive* serve as an easy introduction to my work, and a great way for people to get to know what I do.

As you become even more well known, you might consider offering higher-ticket workshops or live events.

Forming Partnerships

Partnering with other people to offer products, services, courses, summits, or events is a powerful marketing tool. You get the benefit of reaching the other person's audience as well as your own.

- You can consider partnering with someone who provides a service your clients will need that you don't offer, such as website design or Facebook ad development.
- You might partner with someone who does the same thing you do, to offer a bundle or special package.
- A partnership could take the form of developing affiliate relationships with service providers who are aligned with your work and your values.

Becoming a Thought Leader

Writing guest posts for writing sites and appearing on industry podcasts are effective ways of becoming a thought leader—someone who is at the forefront of their industry. They're a good way to get your name out there and to connect with potential clients and influencers.

- Podcasts are a phenomenal way to reach writers. There are hundreds of podcasts directed at writers and creative professionals. Being a guest on a show becomes an evergreen marketing tool—something that is always available and never goes out of date. You get to talk for 30 minutes or an hour about what you do, teach, and tell stories. Most shows have guidelines for pitching; you can start on new shows, or small shows, and work your way up to bigger audiences.

- If you want to start a podcast of your own, that is even more awesome, because you get to control the conversation—but it is also, of course, a lot of work. We started the *Mom Writes* podcast at Author Accelerator to showcase what a book coach does. It's been a fantastic way to drive traffic to our site.

RECOMMENDED RESOURCES

» John Lee Dumas, host of **Entrepreneurs on Fire**, offers **The Ultimate Guide to Podcasting**, a free manifesto to get you started in the world of podcasting. His resources are what host Abby Mathews used when conceptualizing Author Accelerator's **Mom Writes** podcast. Along with an 8-step process for creating and launching a podcast, Dumas talks about equipment, programs, and how to create a quality podcast "without spending a lot of money or being a 'techie.'"

» Pat Flynn at Smart Passive Income also has a step-by-step tutorial called **How to Start a Podcast**.

- Guests posts are also excellent for gaining exposure. A good place to start looking for blogs that take guest posts is the *101 Best Websites* list that *Writer's Digest* puts out each year. Cull through the list, see which sites might be a good fit for your area of expertise, and check out their submission requirements.

   PRO TIP: You can start writing posts on *Medium* whenever you have something to say. There are a lot of channels for writers and creators—look for Books, Fiction, and Writing, among others.

Using a Virtual Assistant

Once your business really gets cooking, you may want to consider using a VA or virtual assistant to help with administrative tasks and organization. There are so many excellent VAs who understand the publishing industry and the world of virtual service providers. I have had good success working with VAs but you have to be extremely clear about what you want and need—how many hours will they work, what technology must they master, what are the tasks you would like them to do?

I recently stepped up and hired a proper executive assistant to help me in my business—a professional who is dedicated to me and my business rather than a VA I am sharing with others. It has been an enormous help as my business has grown.

RECOMMENDED READING

» *The 4-hour Workweek* by Tim Ferriss. Ferriss is a big fan of outsourcing. He takes the idea a bit far in this book, but it's interesting to consider what you can hire other people to help you do.

Self-Care

One of the realities of serving writers who are trying to tap into their emotions and to understand the human condition is that it takes a great deal of emotional, as well as intellectual, energy. Digging into people's stories and arguments, thinking deeply about them, and telling the truth in a compassionate way can be quite draining, and it's easy to burn out.

Nicole Lewis-Keeber is a therapist who specializes in helping small business owners build emotionally sustainable businesses. I love how she frames the conversation. "What kind of relationship do you have with your business?" she asks. "Is it loving and supportive? Or demanding and demeaning?" When you are striving toward success, it's easy to let your relationship with your business become abusive—and that is clearly not the desired outcome.

If you want to continue to do good work, you have to develop a practice of self-care.

Self-care decisions for book coaches should include who you decide to work with, how you set your boundaries, and when you decide to dismiss a writer, but it should also include some sort of awareness and practice for replenishing the well you dip into to help your writers.

Yoga teachers and other healers talk about "holding space" for people—creating a safe space where people can breathe, and rest, and do the work of deepening their practice. What we are doing as book coaches is no different. We need to be aware of the energy we are spending, and mindful of how we are replenishing ourselves.

Self-care for book coaches also extends to physical realities. We spend so much time in our heads as book coaches that it's easy to lose touch with what our bodies need. Take time to tune into your body on a regular basis throughout the day and make sure your environment is designed to give you comfort and ease.

- Do you have a good chair?
- Good lighting?
- Good glasses, if you need them?
- Are you taking breaks from sitting or staring at the screen?
- Are you drinking enough water?
- Are you getting enough physical exercise to counteract all the mental energy output?

Take Action
Write out any thoughts you have on optimizing your business. Even if you won't put these ideas into action just yet, it's good to have them in the back of your mind so you can always be working toward them. Don't forget to include a self-care plan that you can use to remind yourself to take care of you.

RECOMMENDED READING

» *An Invitation to Self-Care* by Tracey Cleantis, LMFT. I coached Tracey on this book, and I love it! It gives a 360-degree view of what it means to be good to yourself, with a lot of practical steps and sample scripts for how to speak to people to set your boundaries and not become a doormat.

Although this is the last section of this book, and very short, I believe it is one of the most important. You can't do good work if you are burned out. You can't seek to delight your clients and be with them down in the muddy trenches of creativity if you are exhausted. You need to be mindful of your limits, aware of your body, and treat yourself with compassion, too.

Helping writers raise their voice and bring their stories to life is *good* work. I love doing it because it feels like a win-win situation—helping someone else with something very important to them feels meaningful and productive and satisfying.

I adore the work, and I hope you do too.

Train to Become a Book Coach

If you'd like to learn more about running a book coaching business, I urge you to sign up for my online self-study master class, *The Business of Book Coaching*. The class covers the same material as this book, but includes 26 videos of me explaining the lessons, more than six hours of awesome in-depth expert interviews, templates from the documents I use to run my multiple six-figure business, spreadsheets to help you determine your prices and manage your clients, bonus downloads, and the chance to join Q&As with me and my Author Accelerator team. You can learn more about this course and receive a discount for having bought this book, at www.authoraccelerator.com/readbooksallday.

You might also be interested in our Book Coach Training and Certification Program, which you can learn about here: www.authoraccelerator.com/book-coach-certification.

Please Leave a Review

If you learned something valuable from this book, I would appreciate your taking a moment to leave a review on Amazon.

Acknowledgments

Thanks to the Author Accelerator team, including Whitney Astbury, Laura Franzini, Terri LeBlanc, Abby Mathews, Diana Renn, Matt Sand, and Lianne Scott for their support and contributions to this book and the accompanying master class. This team makes me better, smarter, and more efficient than I would ever be on my own. I'm so grateful to work with you all.

Thanks to Rosie Nevius and Natasha Vorompiova for helping me get my business (and my mind!) into shape, and to Pam Slim for helping me catch the vision for the transformation.

Thanks to Dan Blank of wegrowmedia.com for our excellent mastermind, where everything gets hashed out every week.

Thanks to Jen Louden for her careful read of these pages; to Michele Orwin for proofreading; to Stuart Bache for the cover; and to Carla Green for the interior design.

Thanks to all my book-coaching clients who taught me far more than I ever taught them.

Thanks to Rob, Carlyn and Emily for cheering me on the journey. I love you guys!

About the Author

Jennie Nash is the founder and CEO of Author Accelerator, a company on a mission to help writers develop the habits, skills and confidence they need to write books worth reading. Her own coaching clients have landed top New York agents, national book awards, and book deals with Big 5 houses such as Scribner, Penguin Random House, Simon & Schuster, and Hachette. She is the author of eight books in three genres. You can learn more at jennienash.com and authoraccelerator.com.

Made in the USA
Columbia, SC
06 January 2020

86462514R00085